Funding Alternatives
for Libraries

Funding Alternatives
for Libraries

Edited by
Patricia Senn Breivik
E. Burr Gibson

American Library Association
Chicago 1979

78349

Library of Congress Cataloging in Publication Data

Main entry under title:

Funding alternatives for libraries.

   "Outgrowth of a workshop...held at the Pratt
Institute Graduate School of Library and Informa-
tion Science in January of 1976."
   Bibliography: p.
   1. Library fund raising. 2. Library finance.
I. Breivik, Patricia Senn. II. Gibson, E. Burr.
Z683.F83   025.1′1   78-27865
ISBN 0-8389-0273-1

Printed in the United States of America

Contents

Preface

This book is the outgrowth of a workshop on fund raising for libraries that was held at the Pratt Institute Graduate School of Library and Information Science in January of 1976. Participants in the workshop included public, academic, and special librarians. The complaint at the end of the two and a half day workshop was that "it wasn't enough." This book is in answer to the concern for more. It is written in recognition of the growing necessity for most libraries to secure funds beyond their primary funding sources in order to maintain current collection development and service patterns, much less to expand.

Updated versions of most of the speeches given at the Pratt workshop are included in this book. Other contributions were sought from people with particular expertise or experiences in library fund raising, and the balance of the book reflects the interaction of a fund raiser who early in her career switched to librarianship and a professional fund raiser who has long had a particular interest in libraries.

Chapter 1

Financial Problems and Some Solutions

Patricia Senn Breivik
and E. Burr Gibson

The financial bubble burst for libraries in the middle 70s. News items concerning slashed budgets and further slashed budgets became, and remain, an almost regular feature in *Library Journal.* Across the country libraries have been tightening their operating, service, and acquisition budget belts and trying to make do with less, but their financial problems are steadily compounded by the reality of both inflation and the information explosion, including the growing concern for the provision of information in all its formats. The biggest problems relating to tax support are in urban areas, where support from property taxes is diminishing. A final contributing factor to the dilemma is the well-documented "inverse relationship between economic prosperity and the demand for services."[1]

The literature documents the coping mechanisms employed by various libraries. They include both negative and positive approaches, plus some that fall somewhere in between, that is, cutting hours of operations and services, charging fees, networking, more attention to legislative lobbying, and increased efforts toward securing grants.

Cutbacks

Cutbacks in a variety of forms were an initial response to the budget slump. One major public library decided to publicize the closing of a branch in a politically active neighborhood, expecting citizen protests to secure additional funding. The plan backfired

1

because the neighborhood quickly perceived that it was being "used." The most frequent approaches were to cut back hours of services, to close one day during the week, to cut back on acquisitions (particularly serials) and/or curtail or eliminate specific services. Unfortunately, such cutbacks were seldom done with much concern for library patrons. For example, it was often the newer services such as outreach, independent study, and the audiovisual programs that were the first to go. Also, public libraries often cut back on weekend and evening hours, which in many cases was a much more convenient way to economize, from a librarian rather than a public point of view.

Other libraries, however, used financial pressures for some serious reexamination of priorities and services. A number of public librarians began urging that more attention should be placed on the outcomes of library programs, not the inputs—that is, size of collections, staff, facilities.[2] One academic librarian warned:

> As librarians, it seems we have been content to *know that* the quality exists while Battle Creek is content if the consumer *thinks* the quality exists. Either way, the consumer loses. The cereal companies must change by putting the quality into the box; the librarian must change by finding new ways to get the quality which is in the box to the consumer.
>
> We must change by shifting some of the emphasis from input to output and apply consumer-oriented standards of quality with greater scrutiny.[3]

Cutbacks also made serious inroads into many library staffs. Even here, however, some attempts were made at more positive solutions. For example, one public library system agreed to try a voluntary reduced work week in order to end a rigid hiring freeze.[4] Other systems, which through personnel freezes or other causes found themselves short of staff, looked to various supplementary sources. Queens Borough Public Library was able to restore five-day-a-week services at all its branch libraries by obtaining 151 CETA (Comprehensive Employment and Training Act) employees,[5] and it actively sought approximately 100 volunteers (some of whom were staff members) to serve as tutors in its Library Volunteers of New York literacy program.[6] Baltimore Public and other libraries followed the example set some years ago by New York Public Library in hiring people with only a bachelor's degree to work in specific areas (e.g., the NYPL subject specialists).[7]

Many people, of course, called such utilization of personnel without library school degrees far from desirable and pointed out the amount of time needed to train such personnel. Such criticism seems to imply that library school-trained personnel need no on-the-job training, and ignores the ALA "Library Education and Personnel Utilization" policy of 1970, which provides for MLS and non-MLS personnel. More importantly, such a negative attitude automatically eliminates one of the few opportunities to maintain services and separate the truly professional tasks from the more clerical.

At least one academic library program was designed by choice— not financial necessity—to free its professionals from many responsibilities normally assigned to librarians so that they might devote their time to reference, collection development, teaching, and librarian/faculty interaction. To accomplish this, Sangamon State University in Springfield, Illinois, has non-MLS college graduates as administrators for its circulation, media, and technical services departments, and civil service staff for its behind-the-scenes operations of cataloging and interlibrary loans. While librarians are not precluded from applying for these positions, they do so under civil service regulations and do not have faculty status.

Networking

Networking and/or library cooperation is often perceived as a means for saving money, and certainly there is much to be gained through such activities. Library literature, however, holds little promise in the way of actual dollar savings; rather it indicates that improvement of services, with greater stability in costs, is more frequently the positive, achieved results. For example, cooperative acquisition programs can help keep pace with inflation. But there are tradeoff costs in expanded bibliographic access and delivery systems, such as potential service slowdown.

Even Big Ten institutions, and others such as Stanford and the University of California (Berkeley), are undertaking "coordinated acquisitions," but the operating price tag is considerable since their cooperative efforts will include

> direct borrowing privileges for faculty, graduate students, and academic personnel at the two institutions; reciprocal lending for all except the undergraduate libraries; delivery intercampus of people and books several times daily; and expansion of Stanford's BALLOTS automation system to Berkeley, "with further network services to other northern institutions."[8]

Indeed, the project is receiving grant support from two foundations, and only experience will prove whether such a cooperative arrangement shows as a plus or minus in the individual institutions' budgets.

However, despite the limited financial benefit, and not withstanding the new copyright law, nothing is likely to thwart expanded interlibrary loan activity in the years to come, with cooperative efforts more frequently crossing the boundaries between types of libraries and between the private and public sectors.[9]

Automation

In terms of saving money, much the same can be said about automation as for networking. Indeed, many of the most promising avenues before libraries today involve networking possibilities made possible by or enhanced by computer-backed technology. Whether on a state, regional, or national level, automated bibliographic and circulation data bases provide service dimensions unthought of not many years ago. So far, however, it has been impossible for libraries or marketing agencies to document dollar savings. This is true about both automated networking activities or automated internal activities such as circulation systems.

It is possible to prove that automation provides better and quicker access to more materials and that checkout/in, reserve, and overdue procedures are more accurate and efficient. Libraries can even point to improved services through more knowledgeable collection development efforts and/or SDI (selective dissemination of information) activities. But it cannot be shown that automation saves money. (Part of the difficulty is, of course, that libraries have never been quite sure what the individual library transactions cost before automation.)

Nevertheless, there is a sound financial reason for automating procedures. While costs related to automation are stabilizing or are dropping, personnel expenditures continue to rise at an alarming rate. Automation, while not an immediate money saver, is a means over the years of slowing down expanding operational costs while also providing better service.

Fees

It is ironic that interlibrary loan activities, which at least are perceived by lay personnel as money saving, are increasingly being eyed as an area for coupon swapping, if not fee charging. Indeed, interlibrary loan fees are currently charged by at least one public library, as well as a growing number of academic libraries.[10]

Currently, the library operation most often accepted as suitable for fee charging is online data base searching, and of course public libraries have long had "pay" duplicate collections of best sellers. Recently, other areas for fee charging have been more actively explored and/or implemented. For example, one Illinois public library is receiving approximately $15,000 per year by renting its audiovisual materials and has seen the use of such material increase 60 percent over the previous year.[11]

Many librarians, however, are strongly opposed to the imposition of any kind of fee, fearing that "at a time when more demands are being made for equal access to education opportunities libraries are seen to be establishing unfair restrictions on access based entirely on the ability to pay for a service."[12] Other arguments against charging fees in public-supported libraries include fear of eroding tax bases and the ethical problem of the fee's being the second charge (on top of taxing).[13]

Lobbying

A possible alternative to cutbacks and fees for publicly supported libraries is more active involvement in the legislative process to build up tax bases. Librarians across the country are attempting to become more politically astute and are increasingly aware of the success or lack of success of ALA and state lobbying efforts. One Oklahoma librarian admonished that, because of the staggering national expenditure for publicly supported libraries, librarians must educate receptive users and legislative bodies to appreciate library needs.[14] Certainly the 1979 White House Conference will offer an unprecedented opportunity to do just that.

Particular promise is presently held for increased state funding for libraries. A recent Commerce Clearinghouse report indicates that states can afford to increase library support, and a 1977 publication of the National Commission on Libraries and Information Science, entitled "Improving State Aid to Public Libraries,"[15] outlines the rationale and justification for the changes. Such changes will be difficult to achieve since they require changes in the state laws and policies. In the case of academic and school libraries, additional state support must usually be won for higher education, and education in general, before the libraries can begin directly competing for funds.

Alternative Funding

Major sources of federal aid cannot be depended upon. An analysis of the federal administration's budget proposals for the Library Services and Construction Act between 1970 and 1976 by the

ALA Washington Office showed a wildly fluctuating and unpredictable situation that has made it increasingly difficult for states and localities to plan effectively.[16] Obviously, national lobbying efforts to date have not been sufficient.

Within these limitations, however, libraries have become increasingly active in seeking funding outside their normal budgetary sources, particularly by approaching federal and state funding sources and private foundations. Indeed, no topic which will be covered in this book has received so much coverage in the literature as that of "grantsmanship"—both governmental and private. Libraries of all types have had varying success in obtaining grants, and librarians are becoming increasingly sophisticated about their grantsmanship activities. However, grants are but one aspect of the larger picture of outside support.

The task of discussing fund raising for libraries is complicated because of differences in the types and sizes of libraries and differences in the types and sizes of their communities. On the other hand, given that specifics will have to vary from library to library, the basic ideas discussed in this book will be applicable in the majority of cases. This book will present a number of possible ways of raising funds for libraries beyond regular budgetary sources and/or income from services rendered, including specific techniques and logistical considerations.

Reference is made to "possible ways" because research indicates that only a few of the nation's libraries carry on a fund-raising program designed to seek gifts on a regular basis from individuals, corporations, foundations, and other private sources of support. For example, the American Association of Fund-Raising Counsel's *Giving, USA* lists and discusses gift support for almost every type of organization and agency except libraries; *Library Literature,* in turn, has subject headings for "grants-in-aid" and "gifts, contributions, etc." but not "fund raising." Despite the fact that today almost every type of institution, whether in the field of education, health, social welfare, or the arts and humanities, is financed in a variety of ways, usually with some mixture of private and governmental support, the number of libraries that seek gifts seems to remain relatively small, even though it is well known that some libraries in fact raise money from private sources on an organized basis.

For example, the New York Public Library raised $3.3 million for operating expenses in 1976-77. One interesting source of support for NYPL in an earlier year was the East New York Savings Bank, which announced that new depositors would have the option of choosing a gift for themselves or having the bank donate the gift's value to the library, after matching this amount with an equal contribution of its own. Each contributor received a certificate in recognition of the contribution, and bookplates bearing the names of donors were placed in the front of the books that were purchased with the money.

Nor is this approach limited to large municipal libraries. Sixteen Atlantic National Banks in Florida participated in a "You're Over-due at the Library" promotion. They offered a $4 donation for each new savings account opened for $100 or more and for each $100 or more added to any existing savings account. Depositors could desig-nate a public school or academic library.

These examples suggest that there *is* a body of potential donors to public libraries who would offer substantial support to many more libraries if potential donors could be *identified, cultivated,* and *asked to give,* and that gift income will be a source of *additional* rather than *substitute* funding.

Another illustration of disinterested private support for a library is the results of a capital campaign conducted by the library in Darien, Connecticut. In this instance over $600,000 was raised from private donors for expansion of the library's facilities, even though there had been no organized fund-raising program prior to the cam-paign. Nearly all of the support came from individuals who were interested in the library, with gifts running to $50,000. While most money came from special gifts, one feature of the campaign was a "phonothon," organized over six evenings, to reach 1,500 general gift prospects, and it brought in over $70,000 to add to the total.

In another campaign, a combination of private gifts (including a "challenge" grant from a foundation) and a special bond issue fur-nished the funds for a new library. Further evidence of the potential for private support can be found in the fact that hundreds of libraries have received gifts from time to time without asking, including bequests.

But what about libraries connected to, or a part of, another institution? We suppose the easy answer is to take the position that the regular development or fund-raising office of the mother institu-tion has the responsibility, and that library personnel should not have to be bothered! A much better plan, however, is for those con-nected with the library to take some initiatives on their own. The initiatives can be directly aimed at funding sources—after clearing (of course) with the development officers in these cases—or the initia-tives may be aimed at the development officers themselves (see chap-ter 13).

There are many situations where special-purpose or special-collection libraries regularly solicit their own boards, and other libraries have developed a Friends of the Library list from which they seek gifts on a regular basis. We have seen other librarians carefully cultivate wealthy alumni or friends of the institution and—again, working through the development office—arrange to have special proposals made for very significant projects. The same things have been done regarding foundation proposals, and in each case the librarian has been a part of the soliciting team.

At this point it may be well to cite the two major causes of negative attitudes toward fund raising on the part of librarians: fear of undermining their regular support base and personal reluctance to ask others for money.

The problem of eroding established funding sources is real; so it is essential to find out whether the board of trustees, institutional managers, or other controlling fiscal agents will permit gift income to be used *over and above* the allocation from the regular budget. This should be settled before any plans are made to secure additional income from gift sources, and certain agreements should be reached on the ground rules to be followed. Nothing would be more frustrating than to expend a great deal of time and effort in launching a fund-raising program, only to see it become a substitute for currently budgeted amounts of money.

It has been said that very few academically oriented people like to help out with fund raising. This reluctance is often expressed in terms of fund raising's not being "professional." In reality, however, much of this reluctance stems from the belief that people don't like to be approached for gifts. The fact of the matter is that millions of people—surely the majority of those able to do so in this country—give to institutions and causes of their choice on a fairly regular basis, and appeals for their support are *expected*. People are hardly ever upset unless the approach is completely tactless or in poor taste.

Further, it is not necessary to be a "salesperson type" to raise funds. All it takes is belief in your program, ability to articulate what you are doing and wish to do and why it is important, and a request for support (usually at a specific level). Indeed, although details of the setting will be different, the process follows much the same steps as those in normal budget negotiating activities, where one is competing for limited funds with other departments or other institutions. The major difference is that library directors *must* compete for their libraries' budgets, but they *may* ignore many alternative funding sources and let them go to others by default. Recent indications, however, point to the fact that, although individual librarians may hang back, the profession as a whole is losing its inhibitions. The overall financial situation for libraries is such that the profession must be ready, actively and openly, to seek all possible funding sources.

There is plenty of money to be given away if the cause is considered worthwhile. Indeed, the American Association of Fund-Raising Counsel's annual report (covering 1976) showed American philanthropy at $29.42 billion, a 9.4 percent raise over 1975.[17] If your cause is better than others, you'll receive preference on the giving list. Money *can* be raised for libraries, but it requires an investment of time and staff.

Fund-raising drives by libraries, however, are still the exception. Beyond increased lobbying and grantsmanship activities, most libraries seem reluctant to engage in major fund-raising efforts. How much longer libraries can afford *not* to explore all possible avenues of funding depends to a great extent on their financial situation and how open their staffs and governing bodies are to cutting back services, utilizing new staffing patterns, and fee charging. This book is written for those libraries and librarians who are dedicated to providing better services to more people and who are, as a means to that end, willing aggressively to explore all financial opportunities which can assist them in their missions.

Notes

1. Jane Hale Morgan, "Dwindling Economy—Booming Library Use," *Michigan Librarian* 41 (Spring 1975): 12.

2. Lowell A. Martin, "User Studies and Library Planning," *Library Trends* 24 (Jan. 1976): 494.

3. Donald F. Webster, "Crunch, Crisis and Change in Academic Libraries," *NYLA Bulletin* 23 (June 1975): 5.

4. "Reduced Work Week Tried by SFPL," *Library Journal* 101 (Nov. 15, 1976): 2332.

5. "CETA at Queens, N.Y.: Five-Day Service Restored," *Library Journal,* 102 (Oct. 1, 1977): 1994.

6. *Library Journal* 102 (July 1977): 1440.

7. "Bachelor's Replacing MLS," *Library Journal* 102 (Apr. 15, 1977): 862.

8. "Stanford & UC Get $$ for Broad-Gauge Co-op," *Library Journal* 102 (Feb. 1, 1977): 320.

9. "Interlibrary Loan: New $$ Constraints & Fees," *Library Journal* 102 (Jan. 1, 1977): 24–25.

10. "Few Academic Libraries Charging Fees," *Library Journal* 102 (Apr. 1, 1977): 752.

11. John Berry, "Editorial: Double Taxation," *Library Journal* 101 (Nov. 15, 1976): 2321.

12. Fay M. Blake and Edith L. Perlmutter, "The Rush to User Fees: Alternative Proposals," *Library Journal* 102 (Oct. 1, 1977): 2006.

13. Berry, "Double Taxation."

14. Mary Esther Saxon, "Libraries Are Involved in the Legislative Process," *Oklahoma Librarian* 25 (Apr. 1975): 9–10.

15. National Commission on Libraries and Information Science, *Improving State Aid to Public Libraries* (Washington, D.C.: Government Printing Office, 1977).

16. American Library Association, *Administrative Budget Proposals Steer Zigzag Course: FY 1970-1977* (Washington, D.C.: ALA, March 1976).

17. American Association of Fund-Raising Counsel, *Giving, USA* (New York: AAFRC, 1977): p. 6.

Chapter 2

Planning for Fund Raising

Patricia Senn Breivik
and E. Burr Gibson

Assuming some interest in embarking on a fund-raising program, what are some of the matters one must consider? Like so many other worthwhile endeavors, a great deal of advance study and planning must take place before a decision is made to move forward. Indeed, serious seeking of funds beyond regular budgetary sources and/or income from services rendered is similar in many respects to other major library operations. First of all, to be accomplished successfully it requires that there be general acknowledgment of the need for fund raising, and placing it among the other operational priorities of the library. Fund raising requires outlays of time and money, and unless there is a reasonable commitment by the staff and governing bodies actively to seek funds, there is little or no chance of success.

For example, growth in a fund-raising program over a period of years can be expected if it is properly structured. This suggests that sometimes the program is not as successful as hoped for in the first year, but if those in charge are persistent, an entirely satisfactory result can be obtained by the second, third, or fourth year, with continuing growth from that point forward. With this in mind, the leadership of an institution should initially make up its mind to make a commitment of at least three years to a fund-raising program before seeking to raise the first dollar. Obviously, no institution would continue a fund-raising program if the first attempt were an absolute disaster, but short of this extreme result, additional patience and additional investment should pay dividends.

For the same reasons, then, that a planning phase should precede the offering of any new service, a serious planning phase should precede the launching of a major fund-raising effort. Agreement should be reached in advance on the direction of the effort, as well as the level of commitment to it. What needs must be met? What outcomes are desired? What resources are available to help reach the desired outcomes? How will success be measured? These and many other questions need to be raised and explored.

Never should a decision be made to get a grant, to develop a friends' group, or have a bake sale before the overall goals of the fund-raising campaign are agreed upon and the overall strategy is planned. Choosing the appropriate avenue of fund raising should be thought of as analogous to choosing the proper teaching methodology after the learning objective, with its evaluative element, has been determined. In most instances, libraries will want to employ a number of different methods in obtaining their fund-raising goals.

Generally speaking, the more an institution invests in fund raising—both in terms of time and supporting materials—the more it can raise. The exceptions usually occur when a very large gift or series of gifts is secured, and it is impossible to plan effectively for them or to build one's operating budget on them.

Planning for fund raising, however, is clearly within the purview of the library director, and this chapter will review the basic steps in such planning. These steps include:

Defining the problem
Developing a plan
    Staffing considerations
    Engaging professional fund-raising help
    Setting objectives and deadlines
    Handling fund-raising expenses
Selecting leadership
Building involvement
Recordkeeping
Reporting back

Defining the Problem

Planning in libraries is not new, nor is self-assessment or priority setting. Community analysis and program evaluations have been done for years. In all these areas ample literature exists to provide guidelines and tools for libraries which are perhaps not quite as far along with their planning skills as others.

The first essential step for fund raising is simply an aspect of basic planning skills, that is, defining the real problems of the library and what is needed to meet those needs. Fund raising is one of the possible means available to the library to meet its defined needs.

Beyond evaluation of the obvious needs confronting the library, preparing for the fund-raising planning process must include consideration of how the public (potential donors) view the library and to what degree they are ready to support a fund-raising campaign in behalf of the library. This may call for a feasibility study. If the results at this point are negative, attention must focus on a public relations campaign, before undertaking fund-raising activities.

The library's self-assessment must also evaluate the availability of leadership to head the campaign, the previous success or failure of fund-raising attempts, and (where appropriate) the degree of institutional or board support for library fund raising. All are elements in defining the problem for fund-raising purposes.

Although library literature on planning clearly encourages broad participation in planning from both library staff and the community, this concept warrants underscoring when planning for fund raising. Wide-based involvement is crucial for three primary reasons. First, a library cannot raise money if the potential donors do not support the purposes for which money is being sought. Second, unless the library staff is supportive, it will be difficult, if not impossible, to maintain an appearance of solidarity and enthusiasm, which is necessary to elicit outside support. Third, from the very beginning it is important to involve the people whom you will look to for leadership both in conducting the campaign and in making some of the leadership gifts. It should be *their* campaign, not the library's.

Agreement among the library staff, institutional officers and/or board members, members of the friends' group, and as large a representation of the general public as possible should be reached on the problems to be met through fund-raising endeavors. Once this agreement is reached, planning can proceed.

Developing a Plan

If responses thus far are fairly positive, a fund-raising plan can be developed. While the plans will vary in size, depending upon the library and the size of the projected goals, six points should appear in every plan:

1. The essence of the case for fund-raising, preferably in the form of a simple summary of the argument rather than any attempt at "deathless prose." This should reveal the aims of the program and the goals for the fund raising, and constitute an official base for all futher utterances.
2. The plan should indicate the basic structure of the campaign, in terms of identification, lines of authority, and forms of committee organization.
3. It should state the requirements in terms of volunteer and paid personnel, card and list systems, office headquarters, campaign literature, necessary equipment, etc.
4. It should lay out standards for giving in the form of tables showing the needed number of gifts of varying amounts, and should specify the workings of some practical quota system by which solicitation can be broken up into manageable local work units, by committees, teams, and individual workers. The quota concept generally is basic to all functions, as a challenge and measurement for performance of any kind.
5. Every plan needs a time schedule.
6. Every plan should have an approved expense budget, with directions for making it work.[1]

Groundwork for the first element in the plan has been laid in the problem defining just discussed, and the Case Statement chapter could be read at this point. The second and third elements in the plan will vary considerably, depending upon the type of library involved (see, e.g., chapter 12, "Operating within a Parent Institution"), the internal staffing available, and whether or not a professional fund-raising council will be employed.

Staffing Considerations

A reasonable expense ratio for fund raising is considered to be around 20 percent of the amount needed, although many agencies (and even colleges) exceed that figure considerably. The annual or capital goal must be fairly high to think about hiring a full-time fund raiser and stay within the 20 percent guideline. By the time a salary is paid for a fund raiser and perhaps part of a secretary's salary, along with materials and postage, the investment easily can run a minimum of $25,000 to $30,000.

Anything less on the projected income side would suggest consideration of a part-time fund raiser, or having an existing staff member take the job. Another alternative would be to hire a professional fund raiser or fund-raising firm, the possibilities are almost endless.

If the amount needed is minimal or the gradual growth concept is embraced, the best alternative is to have staff members take on the job initially and then to add staff as income becomes more substantial.

Depending on the amount to be raised and the availability of funds to invest in the program, the options might be charted as follows:

Staffing Possibilities—Public Libraries or Independent Institutional Libraries

1. Librarian alone, as extra responsibility
2. Librarian plus outside counsel (counseling firm, free lancer, direct mail specialist)
3. Librarian plus help from public relations staff member plus outside counsel
4. Part-time staff member (also responsible for public relations and community relations)
5. Part-time staff member plus outside counsel
6. Fund-raising handled completely by outside counsel
7. Full-time staff member
8. Full-time staff member plus outside counsel
9. Full-time staff member plus resident director from fund-raising firm.

Staffing Possibilities—Institutional Libraries

1. Leave fund raising entirely to development office
2. Librarian takes initiative in fund-raising matters
3. Other library staff member is assigned to take initiative
4. Part-time fund raiser is assigned to library by development office
5. Full-time fund raiser, coordinated with development office.

To a large extent, then, staffing considerations will have to be based upon the size and potential of the fund-raising effort. The ideal situation is to have professional librarians (usually the director) *and* professional fund raisers involved. One of the things that must not be done is to hire somebody to do the fund raising' or get the development office to do fund raising, and then have the librarian have nothing to do with it. People—including corporate and foundation representatives—want to hear from the people who are running the program to which they are asked to donate. They don't want to hear about it from the fund raiser.

The best fund raisers, then, are the "enablers." They are the ones who help form the committees, who help get volunteers and/or the professional staff together with potential donors. They are the ones who do the time-consuming nitty-gritty, but when it comes to actual visitations, as much professional staff time should be set aside as possible.

Engaging Professional Fund-Raisers

Fund raising is a specialized business, and it makes good sense in thinking about a fund-raising program for the first time to consider the possibility of bringing in experts. Obviously, such a move increases the initial investment, but it also substantially increases the opportunity to raise the maximum amount of money. Several types of fund-raising expertise are available, and there are several ways in which a library can work with a fund-raising firm or an independent professional. Some firms and some independent fund raisers specialize in particular types of fund raising, such as direct mail, special events, or securing foundation grants.

A fund-raising firm or an independent consultant could be (1) brought in to do a "market" or feasibility study to help gauge the potential for such a program; (2) requested to establish a fund-raising plan and make suggestions as to how it could be carried out, including a timetable, a copy theme, and types of activities; (3) employed in an ongoing consultation arrangement where the fund raiser would visit on a regular schedule to be sure the appropriate steps are taken in the proper order and proper way; (4) asked to execute the entire campaign (this is often done when a capital campaign is embarked upon); or (5) called in to help with some specific portion of a campaign, such as writing the proposals.

The cost of professional services can run anywhere from a total of a few hundred dollars to a few hundred dollars a month for counseling, or several thousand dollars per month for full-time service.

In negotiating the amount to be paid a firm, the following guidelines from a seasoned fund raiser can be helpful:

All firms worth having are paid a fee, and never a percentage. And their charges are based on the number of men assigned, the duration of the service, and the out-of-pocket expenses involved. Fees for the exploration job and the planning may be figured separately—particularly if the findings are negative, which happens more often than you might suppose, and the proposed campaign has to be cancelled or postponed. But the fee for campaign service will be at the rate agreed upon in advance, win, lose, or draw.[2]

The American Association of Fund-Raising Counsel (AAFRC), which represents the largest of the professional fund-raising firms, has published a promotional brochure which lists the advantages of hiring professional counsel.[3] Just as library consultants are often hired to capitalize on their in-depth knowledge when a new building or other major undertaking is contemplated, a professional fund-raising counsel can call upon its experience and skills to meet specific library needs, taking particular "pride in saving time for volunteers and money for the client."[4] Benefits of good counsel frequently last far beyond the campaigns for which it is employed, as sound and workable fund-raising plans for future, well-established procedures and trained library staff are frequently by-products of the campaigns. Indeed, one standard in choosing a firm might well be its orientation to *help* the library raise money, rather than to raise money *for* the library.

When hiring a counsel, care should be taken to engage its services as early in the planning as possible. Often the counsel's experience can help one avoid otherwise unnoticed pitfalls, and/or it may conclude that a campaign is not feasible at that particular time.

Fund-raising efforts which aim for $100,000 or more should give consideration to hiring professional help, unless a qualified professional is a member of the library or the library's parent institution staff. The fair practice code endorsed by AAFRC can be used as measuring criteria in choosing a counsel. The code is as follows:

> Member firms will serve only those charitable institutions or agencies whose purposes and methods they can approve. They will not knowingly be used by any organization to induce charitably-inclined persons to give their money to unworthy causes.
>
> Member firms do business only on the basis of a specified fee, determined prior to the beginning of the campaign. They will not serve clients on the unprofessional basis of a percentage or commission of the sums raised. They maintain this ethical standard also by not profiting, directly or indirectly, from disbursements for the accounts of clients.
>
> The executive head of a member organization must demonstrate at least a six-year record of continuous experience as a professional in the fund-raising field. This helps to protect the public from those who enter the profession without sufficient competence, experience, or devotion to ideals of public service.

The Association looks with disfavor upon firms which use methods harmful to the public, such as making exaggerated claims of past achievements, guaranteeing results, and promising to raise unobtainable sums.

No payment in cash or kind shall be made by a member to an officer, director, trustee, or adviser of a philanthropic agency or institution as compensation for using his influence for the engaging of a member for fund-raising counsel.

Setting Objectives and Deadlines

Element 4 in the fund-raising plan concerns establishing committees and setting solicitation quotas. These matters are covered in chapter 6, "Fund-Raising Programs," but they also relate intimately with element 4, which establishes a time schedule. Like almost every activity in the library, unless deadlines are set, things never seem to get finished. A timetable can serve as one of the two good check points throughout the campaign—quotas or objectives being the other. Moreover, a time schedule is particularly important in fund-raising since the efforts of so many different people must be coordinated to assure that needed activities take place in the proper sequence and that minimum effort is expended by the professional staff and the volunteers. For example, the promotional campaign should precede the solicitations and coincide with the most active phases of the campaign.

Handling Fund-Raising Expenses

The old phrase "It takes money to make money" is just as true in fund raising as it is in business. Just how much might be needed to meet fund-raising expenses depends on how fast the program would have to be developed.

If, for example, it were possible to allow a number of years for the program to provide amounts equal to 5 to 10 percent of the total budget, a step-by-step process could be formulated to avoid a major investment. One could easily visualize a plan where, in the first year, a relatively small number of prospects—individuals, companies, and perhaps foundations— would be selected, and all of them would be personally contacted. A portion of the collected funds would be set aside for an expanded program the following year, and so on into the future. As larger lists of potential donors were identified, more mail solicitations would have to be used, and higher costs would be anticipated.

On the other hand, if for some reason it appeared to be necessary to make appeals to a fairly large list at the outset, funds would have to be advanced from some source to cover the cost of the program. Seed money could be sought from a foundation or corporation; members of the board could put up the funds if the potential existed; currently budgeted funds might be freed if a volunteer group (such as Friends of the Library) would raise money for an item already in the budget; or community or institutional budget funds might be allocated for fund-raising expenses if a strong case could be made for the additional income that would be generated.

In analyzing the possible potential for a program and thereby getting a feeling for what size of investment would be needed, libraries might turn to professional fund-raising counsel for advice, or consult other agencies and organizations in the community that raise funds.

The safest approach is a gradual one, and it is the approach that should be chosen unless it's a matter of raising substantial sums or perish; but whatever approach is taken, it is important that a budget be carefully planned, not on the basis of some arbitrary percentage but as part of the planning process and to serve as a check on management.

The following checklist can be used in budget planning.

Checklist for Campaign Budget

1. Salaries and Fees
   a. Professional staff
   b. Clerical
   c. Federal deductions
   d. Fees for professional firm, auditors, etc.
2. Organization Expense
   a. Luncheons, dinners, and meetings
   b. Travel
3. Promotion and Publicity
   a. Printed material
   b. Art work
   c. Models and visualizations
   d. Direct-mail costs
   e. Stills and motion pictures
   f. Special-presentation expense
   g. Radio and TV
4. General Expense
   a. Rent
   b. Furniture and fixtures

      c. Business machines
      d. Office supplies
      e. Telephone and telegraph
      f. Postage
      g. Freight and express
      h. Messenger service
      i. Electricity and water
      j. Service and repairs
      k. Insurance
      l. Bank charges and interest
   5. Contingencies[5]

Selecting Leadership

Perhaps the most essential element in any fund-raising program is the willingness of members of the board to take leadership roles, in terms of both working and giving. The willingness of the trustees to enter into fund-raising program can be ascertained by making a presentation to them that outlines the types of activities to be considered, the roles they must play, the expenses involved, and the possible dollar returns. Help for preparing such a presentation could be requested from the executive officers of other agencies or organizations that are already raising runds, or professional counsel could be invited to meet with the board.

Obviously, the type of library and its location will determine to a great extent the kind of fund-raising program that can be considered. If it is a public library in a well-to-do community, the problems will be very different from those of a public library in an extremely poor community or neighborhood. If it is a special-purpose library — perhaps connected to a college or university—an entirely different set of considerations emerges. In a case of the latter, the backing of the president and the development officers is essential, and the friends' group if one exists. School libraries will need the backing of the principals, school boards, and in some cases the parents-teachers organizations.

Regardless of the type of library, however, support and backing from members of the policymaking, financially responsible group is absolutely essential. If the governing members are not willing to work or give to the extent their resources permit, who else can take the lead? John W. Nason, former president of Carlton and Swarthmore colleges, in a study on the future of trusteeship prepared for the Association of Governing Boards of Colleges and Universities, gave the rationale for this principle:

In the long run it is the responsibility of trustees and regents to balance income and expenditures, to reconcile resources with programs. They are in a better position than any other group to preserve the financial health of the institution. They are outside the daily operations which often encourage a myopic view. They stand enough apart to have a certain perspective. They are aware, or should be, of the trends and pressures of society which bear upon the college or university. In public universities they are closer to and more involved in the affairs of the institution than the governor, the budget bureau and the committee on education of the state legislature. Theirs is the final responsibility for the solvency of the institution.[6]

In fact, a good time to begin thinking about fund raising is when there is going to be a change in board membership. To the extent that a library has an independent board and the librarian can influence the makeup of the board, it is useful to keep in mind that personal contact is often invaluable in soliciting gifts. It is helpful to get people on the board who have a broad interest in the community, rather than people who are assumed to have an interest in books. This same principle holds true with school boards, friends' groups, etc.

Early in the planning stage a steering committee should be established which will include key people from the board and/or wider institution membership, chairpersons of the planning sub-committees, and a few representative members of the community at large. This volunteer committee is appointed by and reports to the board, school board, university foundation, or other authoritative body. The director of the library and the development officer and/or fund-raising counsel should be ex-officio members of the committee.

Often it is necessary to have a well-spelled-out case for fund raising before one tries to enlist quality leadership; but from its appointment, and throughout the planning stages and actual implementation of the campaign, the steering committee should be actively involved in all decision making. This committee will also have the important task of helping to recruit top-notch personnel for all the committees which are essential to the success of the campaign.

Besides looking for leadership within the board or elsewhere (close to the heart of the institution), much of the leadership will have to depend on those who have a special interest in the library, that is, members of friends' groups and/or library users. In enlisting leadership, the following advice from an experienced fund raiser should be remembered.

The principle holds true that the place to look for leaders is where public interest ranks high. The new head of a local bank seeking growth, the newcomer who has been brought in to head an important business and needs broad acquaintance and prompt recognition, the young lawyer in quest of favorable visibility within the strictures of his legal ethics, the holder of the district franchise for bottling and distributing popular soft drinks—all these and their comparable counterparts are among the suitable and likely candidates. But whatever the man's ranking and whatever the cause, the main thing to look for here is the kind of natural and honorable motivation that leads to first-class attention.

And this you are most apt to find among those who are always busy and often "too busy." Retired men, in fact, are usually bad risks for hard and effective leadership.[7]

Always try to recruit leaders who could make the largest gifts themselves (rather than someone who could do an awful lot of work but can't make much of a gift). Go for the best leaders available. Do the home work and take the time necessary to secure their participation. Nothing is more important than this.

The number and size of committees will vary according to the size of the library and the campaign that is undertaken. Frequently there will be committees for public relations, prospect file (list) maintenance, special events, speaker programs, and hospitality tours. Eventually there will also have to be a structure (similar to committees') to handle the actual solicitation of funds; often this work will be divided under a major gifts chairperson and a general campaign chairperson.

Many libraries will attest to the ongoing value of many of these committees. Running annual fund drives or friends' membership campaigns can be effectively handled by volunteer committees, as can ongoing programs of public relations and special events. One public library in Connecticut, which serves about 50,000 people and has approximately 400 volunteers on an ongoing basis, has found that a unique *esprit* results from the partnership of the executive committee of the friends' group and the board of trustees in promoting a worthwhile community effort. Such committee work can also produce the leadership for the campaigns of tomorrow, as the chairperson of the library's development committee admonishes:

Do not underestimate [volunteers'] growth possibilities — that the new volunteer may someday be on your board of directors, and any background knowledge acquired from actual experience with your organization will contribute wisdom to these important decisions even years from now.[8]

Good fund-raising tactics not only can build on themselves for improved results in the future, but can help build the library's leadership base for the future.

Building Involvement

The importance of the involvement of library staff and the community in planning for fund raising has already been discussed under the section "Defining the Problem." If a library has been slow in the past to build a broad-based involvement in its program, steps should be taken to improve this situation as quickly as possible. Such efforts should be seen as "the most dependable way to develop advocacy and support at the maximum level, preferably all the time but especially in the pre-campaign period."[9] Things as simple as asking for advice or opinions, and really listening, are good first common-sense steps. The aim is not that the campaign be the library's campaign, but the campaign of as many people as possible.

Recordkeeping

The final matter that should be considered in planning a fund-raising program is the absolute necessity of keeping good records. Often the importance of recordkeeping is thought of only after the fact or, in the case of governmental or foundation grants, when reports are required.

Almost all good fund-raising techniques are capable of showing increases year after year with proper planning and follow-through. This growth process, however, cannot take place unless a good set of records is maintained. In order to ask a prospective donor—whether an individual, corporation, or foundation—to increase a gift, there must be a record of what was given in the past. If a donor wants to check a gift record with the institution, nothing can be more devastating than to find that no such record exists! Good recordkeeping, then, is an absolute prerequisite for an ongoing and successful fund-raising effort.

The recordkeeping system can begin as the fund-raising system begins—on a limited basis and with a fairly simple format—and can grow as the fund-raising program grows. However, there are three necessary elements in the beginning recordkeeping system.

First, there is the gift ledger, which shows the date of a gift, the name of the donor, the amount of the gift, and any designated use specified by the donor, The receipts for the day or week should be arranged in alphabetical order by donor and posted in the general ledger under the suggested headings, and a total should be placed at the end of the listings. The gifts should be totaled on an adding machine, and the tape, along with the checks and cash, should be transmitted to the treasurer of the institution for deposit. A copy of the deposit slip should be returned to the desk of the person who keeps the records, to be attached to that page of the ledger.

Second, a 4-by-6 card should be prepared for each donor and should include the full name and address, as well as some kind of identification as to the type of donor (board member, library card holder, corporation, etc.), and a set of boxes should be provided in which to note the date and the amount of the gift, with perhaps a line for subtotals that show the total gifts to date. There should be extra space in file-card drawers so that as gifts come in and are posted to the cards, the cards can be moved from one file to another—those remaining in the original file representing the regular donors who have not yet responded to your appeals. This file can be used for follow-up purposes as your campaign proceeds

File cards should be tabbed to indicate certain classes of donors, either by the source or the size of the gift. A gift-acknowledgment form should be devised so that every donor may be assured that the gift has been received. A common practice is for a letter of acknowledgment to be sent to all donors who have made gifts of a certain size, with perhaps a well-designed printed acknowledgment for all gifts up to that amount. The printed acknowledgment can also be signed personally by the director of the library or the person in charge of the fund-raising program, and if letters are used, they should be typed individually. An exception to the standard letter should be made each time a gift is of such significance that the director feels an individually dictated message is in order. Care must also be taken with follow-up activities, such as bookplates or plaques.

Third, individual file folders should be prepared to hold the correspondence that may be generated in the acquisition of gifts. Very often, gifts from corporate sources will come in with correspondence, as will gifts from foundations and sometimes from individuals.

As the volume of recordkeeping increases, it will soon be necessary to set up Addressograph plates or some similar system, to be used when later appeals are sent. It is now very possible to call upon a computer service house to punch this information on cards and run sets of labels or envelopes as the need arises. This is the simplest use of a computer, and it can often be done for less than installing an Addressograph system. As the years go by and the donor list grows into the thousands (for large library constituencies), consideration will need to be given to whether the entire set of gift records should be computerized. As a rule of thumb, this rarely has seemed to make economic sense until the donor list has grown to 10,000 or more names, but technological advances are making the computer handling of smaller lists quite economical.

Samples of recordkeeping forms can often be obtained from previous community campaigns, development offices, and printed materials. The *KRC Fund Raiser's Manual* contains a number of such examples.[10] As fund raisers have long known and library literature is beginning to reflect, "How often donations are made may depend on what happens after the money has been given."[11] Good recordkeeping is an essential ingredient in successful ongoing fund raising.

Reporting Back

Recordkeeping, as has been pointed out, is required for having the information necessary to respond to donors' queries and to know at what level to request future gifts. Keep in mind that once a donor gives $50 or $100 a year, there is an excellent opportunity to receive as much as $500 or $1,000 annually, if, over a period of years the donor is kept informed and feeling needed. Communicating with donors (i.e., reporting back to them) is essential to such growth in support.

Reporting back can take many forms: announcements at special events, through published sources as news releases; annual reports and newsletters, through specially prepared reports; and individual conversations or correspondences. Nothing succeeds in fund raising like success, and you want donors to be kept appraised of progress that is being made as well as needs left unmet.

Obviously, at the end of a major campaign a final report should be prepared for internal and external use. Care should also be given to follow-up reports to foundations, even if they are not required. The library may want to approach the same foundation in the future.

Reporting back also has a great deal to offer in the actual running of the campaign. During the campaign, reporting back helps assure that objectives and quotas are being reached on schedule and that the entire campaign remains synchronized. Everyone is familiar with "thermometers" and other display devices which can foster a team-like (albeit competitive) spirit as goals are neared. It is also most important regularly and frequently to acknowledge and reward the work and successes of campaign workers. This form of reporting does much to foster the morale of the volunteers and, ultimately, promote the success of the campaign.

Notes

1. Harold J. Seymour, *Designs for Fund-Raising* (New York: McGraw-Hill, 1966), p. 40.

2. Ibid., p. 175.

3. The brochure *Some Reasons Why* can be obtained by writing to the American Association of Fund-raising Counsel, 500 Fifth Avenue, New York, N.Y. 10036.

4. Ibid., p. 5.

5. Seymour, *Designs,* p. 88.

6. "The Future of Trusteeship" (Washington, D.C.: Assn. of Governing Boards of Colleges and Universities, 1974).

7. Seymour, *Designs,* p. 49.

8. Amedee J. Cole, "Volunteers—And How They Serve!" in *KRC Handbook of Fund-Raising Strategy and Tactics,* ed. Joseph A. Ecclesine (Mamaroneck, N.Y.: KRC Books, 1972), p. 16.

9. Seymour, *Designs,* p. 42.

10. Paul Blanshard Jr., ed., *KRC Fund-Raiser's Manual: A Guide to Personalized Fund Raising* (New Canaan, Conn.: KRC Development Council, 1974), pp. 218–26. See also the narrative on pp. 77–82.

11. Bruce Berney, "Northwest Libraries Report: Encouragement of Gifts and Memorials," *PNLA Quarterly* 41 (Spring 1977): 25.

Chapter 3

Public Relations and Publicity

Patricia Senn Breivik
and E. Burr Gibson

Acknowledgment of the importance of libraries' having ongoing programs of public relations has been growing in acceptance for a number of years, particularly among public librarians. This acceptance has serious implications for fund raising. Libraries which have well-developed public relations programs should find fund raising to be a natural outgrowth of their PR activities, while other libraries may find themselves in a position of having to delay fundraising activities until an adequate public relations program can be established.

Preparing for his presentation at the Pratt Institute on fund raising for libraries in 1976, one of the professional fund raisers made a special trip to the public library, which he and his family frequently used, in order to take a fresh look at a familiar place. Much to his surprise, he found a number of services were offered which he had previously never noticed, including an extensive record collection. His admonishment, as expressed to the institute participants on the need for public relations, was based on personal experience.

There is no more frequent cause for postponing needed fundraising activities than lack of knowledge on the part of the community as to the activities of the library and how these activities are meeting real needs which its community is facing. Stereotypes of libraries and librarians need to be expelled and individuals and companies educated on how libraries of today are serving their interests. This is equally true for libraries which are part of larger institutions.

Public relations, of course, is much broader in its scope than publicity. It includes news releases and all other publicity pieces, but public relations also has to do with how patrons are treated when they call or come to the library, special events, organized friends' groups, how complaints are handled, and a multitude of other daily occurrences. Public relations has alternately been called a state of affairs and a way of life.

Public relations by its very nature, if well done, promotes giving. When one is preparing to launch a major fund-raising campaign, however, special efforts should be taken and publicity produced which is aimed at educating potential donors on the record of the library to date, what its current needs are, and how they can help. The chief tool in this process is called the "case statement," and the following chapter focuses on what goes into a good case statement and how it can be used.

Beyond the case statement, however, are many public relations activities which can undergird fund-raising activities. These are outlined in the *KRC Fund Raiser's Manual* and include establishing a good picture file, establishing an ongoing program of news releases, writing feature articles, producing series of letters aimed at top prospects, providing spot interviews and feature-style documentaries for radio and television, sponsoring hospitality tours of the library, and establishing a slide-tape program which can be used by speakers and in organizing special events. Obviously, a full-blown public relations campaign will require a great deal of work, careful coordination, and probably the establishment of a number of committees.

The emphasis of the library's public relations program, with the support of fund-raising efforts, should be somewhat different initially than three or four years down the line. Initially it might have to heavily stress why money from gifts is needed, even though most of the support is from the tax dollar. This could even be made a question: Why does the library need money when it gets financial support from taxes? Then, as the fund-raising program grows (when some people give, the library's case becomes more acceptable to others, and the library can prove that if some people give, other people ought to), the emphasis can switch to the outstanding record of the library to date, its current needs, new services it wants to offer, etc. The question is how much does somebody know about the library when you want to start talking about specific needs. If they don't know it well, the public relations effort will have to start from the beginning and make the argument as to why people ought to give to a library in the first place.

In libraries that already have a public relations officer, care should be given to how this person relates to the key development officer. Their efforts must be coordinated. As one public relations/development officer wrote:

> Any organization which raises money or plans to raise money, has to lay the groundwork through a public relations program, even in the beginning. You must educate your public to give. You must supply them with positive information on a continuous basis. This continuing information program will, in turn, become the basis for a continuing development program.[2]

How to develop a public relations program and good publicity is the subject of many books, articles, courses, and workshops. Just as there are professional fund-raising firms, there are numerous public relations firms and free lancers available for hire by libraries. Other possibilities which should not be overlooked are securing donations of such skills from organizations—if not those which specialize in such services, then the public relations and/or publicity departments of companies—and the talents available from staff and (on a volunteer basis) the community. Certainly in setting up publicity committees, representatives from local newspapers and broadcasting stations should be included, plus public relations officers from local firms.

Sometimes what is needed is perspective and imagination to see how certain ongoing library activities can be used for public relations and, through public relations, fund raising. For example, Harold Seymour, dean of the fund-raising profession, admonishes:

> The average annual report in the voluntary field, in the opinion of far too many, is still so steeped in tradition that readers are repelled rather than attracted. And this is a great pity indeed. For as all modern corporations now know so well, the annual report should be the institutional voice at its very best, with every good chance of reaching and influencing the best part of the constituency.[3]

A number of public relations–minded librarians also support the importance of the annual report as a primary tool in gaining better financial support. In an article entitled "Effective Library Promotion Builds Better Financial Support," the author contends that "if the library can afford only one major public relations effort, it may be worthwhile to concentrate on the presentation of the annual budget or report."[4]

A library should not give donors all of the complex detail that its governing board may require, but rather point out the major categories. In essence, the library should very briefly say: These are the services the library performs, and we think that as one of its supporters you'd like to know. A survey on annual reports[5] found that about 87 percent of the people who receive annual reports from organizations at least look them over. It said that 75 percent prefer a very simple, clear report. They desire brevity and clarity. This certainly is one easy way to continue to build support for the library over the years.

No consideration of public relations activities in support of fund raising could be complete without mention of friends groups. Friends groups have been valued allies of libraries for many years. As one article summed up, friends groups fall into three categories:

> Those that are building and developing a library for their community, those that assist in the administration of a library, and those that provide volunteers, financial assistance, and communication to the general public. Most Friends organizations fall into the last classification, but all three types can be useful to their libraries in a myriad of ways.[6]

The principal functions of most groups are to help change the image of libraries and librarians, to help libraries communicate with their communities and with government, and to raise money.

Obviously, the interrelationship between public relations and fund raising is nowhere clearer than in the concept of friends groups, and it will be to the members of this group that the library will want to look for assistance in planning for fund raising, for staffing the necessary campaign committees, for approaching prospective donors, and for lead off contributions. Remember, the more one is involved with an organization, the more one thinks of it as his/her organization, and the greater the contribution one is likely to make.

All aspects of public relations demand ongoing commitments of time and money, but friends groups in particular require a great deal of ongoing commitment from the director of the library or someone close to the top. If one is fortunate enough to have a dynamic self-starter as president of the friends' group, the demands will probably be as great but they may prove to be more productive financially.

A good example of how a friends group can build up its contribution to a library over a period of years is given in chapter 14, but almost every librarian has had some firsthand experience with friends groups.

It is possible to have an effective public relations program for a library without being actively involved in fund raising, but it is not possible effectively to raise funds for a library if a good public relations effort is not operating as backup.

Notes

1. Paul Blanshard Jr., ed., *KRC Fund Raiser's Manual: A Guide to Personalized Fund Raising* (New Canaan, Conn.: KRC Development Council, 1974), pp. 41–52.

2. Seymour Leon, "Development and Public Relations—Must the Twain Meet?" in *KRC Handbook of Fund-Raising Strategy and Tactics,* ed. Joseph A. Ecclesine (Mamaroneck, N.Y.: KRC Books, 1972), p. 28.

3. Harold J. Seymour, *Designs for Fund Raising* (New York: McGraw-Hill, 1966), p. 166.

4. Michael Starry, "Effective Library Promotion Builds Better Financial Support," *PNLA* 38 (July 1974): 17.

5. Robert H. Lewis, "Attitudinal Survey Reveals Donors View of Fund Raising," *Fund Raising Management* 5 (Nov.–Dec. 1973): 24–28.

6. Paul T. Scupholm, "The Library's Friends—Their Responsibility to the Community . . . and the Library," *Michigan Librarian* 41 (Spring 1975): 11.

Chapter 4

The Case Statement

Donald A. Miltner

In preparing for fund raising, as discussed in the chapter on planning, you will have to determine your own readiness in terms of the elements essential for successful fund raising. Requirements will include careful examination or self-study, analysis of your findings, and creation of an initial plan for action. Finally, you will want to refine that plan into a final course of action and present it in a document called a case statement.

Your institution will have considerable flexibility with regard to packaging your case statement. That determination will depend largety upon the type of fund-raising program undertaken and the character of your institution. What a strong case should include, however, is considerably less flexible.

What is a case statement, and just what should it accomplish? First, it should serve to create awareness of your institution. You would be amazed if you knew how few individuals know only the name of your institution or where you are located, and little else. Second, a good case should provide understanding of your institution: its history, purpose, philosophy, and achievements—all the information essential to basic understanding. Third, it should motivate the reader to consider positive action by presenting a dynamic picture of what your institution could accomplish if specific plant, personnel, and programmatic needs were provided. Last, it should personally involve the reader in advancement of your institution by asking for a specific commitment.

A case statement is the one fund-raising publication that can afford to be lengthy, because it must be complete. No prospective substantial donor will consider making a significant commitment until he or she has a thorough appreciation of your institution, its objectives, and the rationale for its needs. Your case statement, therefore, is your most essential fund-raising tool, upon which all other communications should be based. It is not merely a tool for capital campaigns but one that is needed *at all times* by any nonprofit institution.

Most good case statements are the end result of a thorough reappraisal of where an institution is in relation to its true goals and its relationship to the publics it is designed to serve. To be effective, a self-study must be boldly honest—pinpointing both strengths and shortcomings in relation to your institution's stated goals. It should involve the participation of key constituents who are representative of your entire constituency, and result in a plan of action that will bring your institution closer to its real goals. It must address the question of cost, in terms of personnel and dollars necessary to implement the plan. It is at this point that your institution will have to make a financial commitment if it is to initiate a fund-raising program. And it should be emphasized that this commitment will have to be made in advance, and sufficient amount, to implement the agreed-to plan.

Specifically, what should a case statement include? It should start with a statement of what your institution is. Most often your own people have a fuzzy and/or different understanding of precisely what your institution is all about. If they do not thoroughly understand your institution, you cannot expect individuals less directly involved to understand it. In depicting your institution you should state what its purpose is, what its philosophy is in carrying out this purpose, what its heritage is, what characteristics of your institution appeal to your specific constituencies, and what makes it unique.

Your statement should be honest, up to date, and written in straightforward language. It should be realistic and relate your institution's goals to the needs of today's society. It will be necessary to examine your statement of purpose periodically to make sure that it remains current and valid.

Your philosophy should be stated in terms of achieving your purpose and in relation to the constituency you seek to serve.

In stating your heritage, you have an opportunity to review the history of your institution. This will enable you to highlight the unique contribution your institution has made, which differentiates it from similar institutions to prospective donors.

An institution always appeals to its various constituencies in different ways. This will come out in the self-study and should serve as a guide to presenting the special characteristics of your institution.

While there are many people who do not know exactly what your institution is about today, many more have little or no knowledge of the many aspects of your institution's program. To these people a library is a library—and, more than likely, as it functioned twenty-five years ago. To capture the interest of this group, it will be necessary to communicate all that your library does, how well it does it in relation to similar institutions, and how it does *not* function as it did twenty-five years ago.

You will have to communicate your programs effectively, the caliber of your people who enable you to carry out your programs, your record of service to the community, how you benefit the larger community today (as well as how you have improved and expanded your program), and, if you have improved your physical facilities over the years, your record in financial management and where your institution stands today in relation to its basic purpose. These are some of the important subjects; undoubtedly you will want to include others which relate uniquely to your situation.

Soundness of program is the foundation on which an effective fund-raising effort can be built, and it is in this critical area that libraries have unique advantages. (I sense, however, that few institutions have been so taken for granted or have operated with such a low profile in our society.) Simply communicating your program and services to your publics will impact pleasantly on many of them.

It is necessary to relate these programs and services to the uses of your various constituents. Because your personnel is specifically trained to provide the services required by your various publics, you should identify such expertise and specifically relate it to the services performed. You have provided unique service to your community over the years, and many of these services relate to special groups such as businessmen, civic groups, and others who might take an interest in seeing your service to them continue and grow.

It has been proved over and over again that donors want to support a winner. If you can show that through hard work and astute stewardship of gifts, as well as other limited resources, your institution has continually upgraded its facilities, your publics will be considerably more inclined to support future physical improvements. In your local community, it is effective to point out that improved physical facilities have added to the beautification and prestige of the community, as well as contributed to improved services.

While few prospective donors request a detailed financial report, most want assurance that your institution is managed efficiently and that it has a genuine sense of stewardship. For this reason it is important to indicate where your money comes from and how it is allocated. Donors appreciate being provided this kind of information without having to ask for it. A summary of your current financial status, convincingly documenting a consistent record of growth, can be particularly effective when graphs are included that project the years ahead.

The next major section of your case should cover the direction your institution must take in the future. It is in this section that you will present the needs for the future which will enable your institution to take the strides that it must if it is to fulfill its objectives in the years ahead. At this point it is necessary to describe in some detail the new directions your institution must take. It is prudent to present future growth as an extension of past achievements, so as not to offend past supporters. In fact, it is a good idea to strongly reaffirm the preservation of the positive qualities of the past that have contributed to the institution's current strength.

To achieve your institutional goals in the years ahead and to keep pace with the trends of the times, you must define the new programs that will have to be inaugurated. The rationale for each new program must be provided in a highly interesting manner. It should appear so essential that interested persons would want to become involved and provide support. Remember, this is the purpose of your case statement.

What new personnel will you need to staff new programs, to replace retiring staff, to strengthen existing programs? What will be required to retain your existing personnel? Precisely what new physical facilities does your institution need to replace outmoded structures, to create space for new programs, to serve a growing constituency? All these questions must be addressed.

Until you decide to go into a building campaign, a general description of why it is needed, and what it will provide, will suffice. However, sketches of any planned new buildings go a long way toward strengthening your case.

Have you considered seeking the undergirding required for the long-range financial stability of your institution through endowment support? If you haven't, you should. Needs for endowment for programs, plant, and personnel are essential to a complete case. More and more institutions are seeking funds for the future operation and maintenance of new buildings as they are erected. Such support reduces the burden the sudden increase in operating funds for any new building brings.

If your institution has recurring needs which you feel could logically be included in your case, do so. You will often be surprised by what interests a specific donor.

In the section on needs, your case statement must make a case for each item. You will have to be prepared to detail these needs for specific proposals. In explaining the reason for each need, it is essential to put emphasis on some negatives. It is virtually impossible, for example, to build a strong case for higher salaries if you do not first prove that present salaries are inadequate. Don't let the thought of negatives worry you; if there were no negatives, you would not need a case statement. It is necessary, however, to balance each negative with a positive. With regard to salaries, give this point a positive aspect by showing your staff to be exceptional and by relating that you have been able to retain the people primarily because of their dedication to your institution. But such dedication has its limits, and it is unfair to ask any person to work for a fraction of their true worth.

In creating your plan for fund raising, it is necessary to assign to each project a target date for completion. This schedule should be realistic, but not so futuristic that a prospective donor loses the feeling of immediacy. These dates are goals which reflect your overall plan. Undoubtedly they will be adjusted, but they are nevertheless essential. In determining your calendar, you will certainly want to consider priority needs (not every project can have equal importance). This is the place to include data from your physical and/or programmatic master plan.

The cost of each project is frequently included with the description. This is not necessary, but somewhere in your case statement there should be a cost breakdown for each project.

In determining costs, you will want to consider a realistic estimate for each project, including a factor for inflation. What are the projects which would alleviate operating income that you will want to include? To realize your needs, what is the range of gifts required? To realize your goals, what must each constituency give? What methods of giving are acceptable? Will you include annual, capital, and deferred gifts in your plan? What are the memorial gift opportunities?

If your process has been comprehensive, covering the points outlined in this chapter, you will be in a good position to enlist the best possible leadership—the most critical ingredient to successful fund raising.

In closing, perhaps a word about "packaging" case statements should be added. Once you have all the needed information, how should it look? Case statements from other institutions may give you some ideas, but just as the information and plans in the statement are unique to the individual library, so too should the packaging of the statement reflect your library. Is your library in a dynamic inner-city situation or is it a research library with hundreds of years of tradition behind it? Obviously, the statements for these libraries should vary in both verbal and visual content.

If you are launching a major capital fund drive, an expensive bound document may be called for, but if the statement is planned for use over a long period of time, a loose-leaf binder may prove much more useful, as sections can be updated as needed. In fact, a multicolor, picture-filled case statement, which might be very appropriate for a large academic library, might be seen as presumptuous and overly expensive for a small district library. A well-thought-out and carefully laid out mimeographed or photocopied statement can be every bit as effective as a more elaborate piece, and almost every library has someone on its staff (or a friend) who has graphic talents which can be called upon.

As has already been said, building plans, where available, can be most useful for interesting donors, and other visuals, carefully chosen to highlight a need or a future building or program, can serve to highlight and give emphasis to the main points in the statement. Graphs and diagrams can effectively illustrate growing financial needs, increased public services, etc. If a symbol is closely identified with your library or parent institution, it too should be utilized.

However the case statement is finally packaged, it should be given out as part of a personal contact whenever possible, so that various sections can be emphasized in response to a prospective donor's stated interests. A follow-up letter can provide additional information on high-interest programs. The case statement can also be sent out with a covering letter to prospective donors and/or foundations. In this case, the letter should point out how known interests of the prospective donor relate to the programs in the case statement, and perhaps highlight one or two items which may be of particular interest.

Finally, if the amount of time and effort needed to produce a good case statement seems high, remember that it is the foundation document from which all other publications can be developed. It not only will provide the information which will be of concern to all major donors—individuals, corporations, and foundations, but it can also be used to help elicit leadership for the campaign and to serve in training and back-up for your volunteers.

A good case statement is one of the most important tools your library can have in seeking outside funding.

Chapter 5

How to Say It

Ellen Barata

It may be the most stimulating, the most exciting fund-raising event of the century. It may be sponsored by the library with the most integrity in the land. It may have been planned to pay for the most pressing need in that library, so pressing that it is obvious to one and all. But without publicity, no one will know about it, no one will come, and not one cent will be raised.

Several points should be established immediately concerning the library's approach to publicity, whether publicity in general or publicity specifically related to fund raising. There is constant lament in the library world about the "mousey" librarian image, but too often there is lament only, and no action to reverse the image. Publicity for fund raising is a good place to begin the action.

Too often the fund-raising appeal is merely "gimme." It is just as easy to say, "Look at all the library gives you. Support this fund-raising event, and you'll get even more from the library."

Another negative approach to avoid in library fund raising is, "The library needs thus-and-so [more space, a film collection, whatever]." It is not the *library* that needs anything, it is the library user; and it is time it were so presented: "*You* need more space, you *deserve* more space, and the library can give you more space if you support this library appeal."

There are two other points to be made for the positive approach. A long recital of the woes of the "poor library," which gives the impression that the institution is down to its last dime, is not only unappealing, it is forbidding. People like winners and they like to be associated with winners; everyone hopes to be on the winning side. If a library is in dire straits, giving to the library seems like pouring good money after bad. A prospective donor might rather give to the high school boosters' club, because the football team won eight out of nine games last season. In short, they are winners.

A second point is that libraries face fierce competition. No one has to prove that a fireman is needed, or a policeman, or a hospital. But libraries have their back to the wall, and a more aggressive approach—a positive approach which accents what libraries give— makes for more successful fund raising.

Elsewhere in this book consideration is given to "building" donor lists; sometimes the list will be the whole community, all alumni, etc. In general, however, the natural audience for any fund raising is the group which will benefit most from the project for which funds are sought. For example, if an expanded music collection is needed in an academic library, the fund-raising list would be headed by professors and graduates of the music department and the local music associations and their members. On the other hand, if the city needs a new branch or expansion of the main library because all services are cramped and crowded, the library will go to the whole community in a general fund-raising effort.

Once the audience is determined, select the media which will reach the most people. Most of these media are available to libraries: newspapers and magazines, radio, television, signs, billboards, posters, and direct mail. Other channels for communicating the fund-raising message include open houses, meetings at the library, and meetings of other groups in the community to which the library can send speakers. In most cases the publicity should utilize a number of media.

Newsletters offer many opportunities for promoting fund-raising activities. The mailing list, directed to the proper audience, is of primary importance. A newsletter can be a very special tool, not only in fund raising but in all of a library's public relations.

One library in New England, knowing an expansion fund drive could not be put off many years longer, began publishing a newsletter. The first issue preceded the anticipated fund-raising kickoff by two years and the early issues were used to acquaint library users with all the services and materials available to them at the library. Having solidified a loyal constituency, the fund-raising campaign got under way after the need had been explained, and progress reports were given in the newsletter every step of the way. Now, six years after the first issue, with the expanded library in full operation, the newsletter continues to convey the library story to its users.

The local newspapers are probably the most frequently used channel of communication. While radio and television have cut into newspaper readership, the papers still give more complete accounts and are the source of amplification and verification of information heard or seen on radio and television.

Magazines can be considered at the same time as newspapers, since many of their requirements are similar. Writing for magazines, however, is not so terse. And magazine deadlines are usually many weeks earlier than the magazine's publication date; so only long-term fund-raising projects or unusual projects of general interest are apt to be accepted as subjects for magazine articles. Fund-raising events may be listed in area-wide magazines if the publications include a calendar of regional activities.

The library should learn all it can about the newspapers and magazines in its area in which stories might be placed, whether they are about fund-raising projects or other events in the library. It is important to know the deadlines of daily, Sunday, Saturday, weekly, and monthly papers and magazines, and also of special supplements. Sometimes these supplements are published near holidays. The newspapers in some communities might also print an annual supplement about all city or civic organizations, and this is a good spot to mention a new library fund-raising project or to report progress on a fund-raising effort already under way. Usually the various sections of the larger papers have a number of different deadlines and it is wise to know them all; if your story is too late for one section, it may be on time for another suitable section with a later deadline.

Although the library may know the mailing address of the newspapers in the area, it should also know the locations of the papers' drops for hand-delivered news releases. This is particularly important if the most-read paper in your community is published in another town and a local correspondent is assigned to your area. There will be more time to prepare a story or add a late development if, instead of mailing it to another city, it can be dropped off at the home or office of the local correspondent. Be sure to know these correspondents' deadlines, which will undoubtedly be different from those at the papers' main office.

Develop person-to-person newspaper and magazine contacts. It is acceptable practice to mail a release to the "city editor" or "sports editor," for example, but it is better to mail it to the specific *person* who is the city editor or sports editor. Better still, make personal contact with the city editor, women's editor, sports editor, the person in charge of the calendar of events, or special-interest writers of columns on topics such as round-the-town, books, or food. When personal contacts are made, ask the best time to get in touch with the people. Nothing can kill a story faster than to toss it at an editor one minute before his or her deadline on a busy day. Two minutes after the deadline, when the rush is over and the editor is relaxed, you might be promised two columns and a picture.

Since pictures are important, it is good to know if a staff photographer is available to cover events originating in the library and, if so, how much notice the paper requires. Is there someone in particular to talk to about pictures? Some newspapers and magazines will accept photos other than those of staff photographers. If so, the library will have to know if these photos should be "glossies" or another finish, what sizes photos can be, is a Polaroid photo acceptable, and are color or only black-and-white photos used? Publications often have their own rules, a common one being a limit on the number of persons they will have in a picture. Deadlines for photos (which may require more processing) are frequently different from deadlines for copy. Some newspapers will return photos, but may require that they be accompanied by a stamped, addressed photo-mailer.

There was a time when a well-written news or feature story, prepared according to a newspaper's rules and sent from the library or another reliable source, would often pass through the editor's desk to the print shop and appear in the next edition as submitted. These days, when many papers are computerized and many others are printed by offset, there is more chance of alteration since every word in these papers must be input into computers or retyped for photographing. Nevertheless, there's still a good chance a release will go through with few changes if it has been written in proper newspaper form.

As to content, newspapers want the five W's and one H—who, what, when, where, why, and how—in as few sentences as possible at the beginning of the story. The most important and most interesting information should come first, with details and elaboration later. If the paper is crowded and only part of the story can be used, the story will be cut from the bottom up — from the end of the story to the beginning. "Interesting information" is something that will attract and pull the readers into the story. Two of the most overworked and useless beginnings in the English language must surely be "The Big City library will ..." and "There will be ..." Neither is in any way distinctive, and could be used to open almost any story. Worst of all, they're dull.

Instead of writing "The Big City library will try to raise money for the reading garden's flowers and shrubs," or "There will be a fund-raising event in the Big City library," try:

> Tulips and daffodils will bloom in the Big City library's "reading garden" in the spring, according to Jane Jones, library director. Ms. Jones made her prediction in announcing an Oktoberfest to be scheduled on the town green from 7 to 10 p.m. October 1. Proceeds will go toward refurbishing the reading garden on the south side of the library.

Generally, newspaper releases should have short and simple sentences in short paragraphs. The columns are narrow; so long paragraphs make big, solid, forbidding blocks of black type.

In submitting a news release, typewrite and double-space the copy on an 8½ x 11-inch sheet of paper, and never, *never,* send a carbon or an obvious photocopy. An editor wants to think he or she is getting the *only* copy, not one of a dozen. Type your name, address, and phone number (single spaced) in the upper left-hand corner. The subject of the release can also be put at the top left-hand corner in capital letters, and in the same place on succeeding pages, followed by the page numbers in arabic numerals. (If you prefer, you can put a headline in capital letters just above the story. The editor will probably change it to fit the newspaper's columns, but your headline will have indicated the gist of the story.) Also, type the release date (if it is important) at the top: FOR IMMEDIATE RELEASE or FOR RELEASE JANUARY 1, 1979.

Unless a news release is very important, it should not run to more than two pages, and preferably only one. Feature stories may run much longer and can be written more informally. Paragraphs should not run over from one page to the next, even if this means leaving a lot of blank space at the bottom of a page, and "MORE" should be typed at the bottom of a page in capital letters if another page follows.

There are many tricks in the trade of writing for newspapers, not the least of which is using "everyday language." To a librarian, this would mean writing that books are "checked in" and "checked out," not "circulated." Most libraries have books on news writing; in fact, if the person who is given this responsibility is a novice, try a book in the children's department of a public library first. Several are excellent and include all the basics, without swamping the beginner in technicalities.

A final suggestion regarding newspaper and magazine writing: It is important to be familiar with the practices of the publications to which the library will be sending material. The large papers and magazines have "style books" which give the preferred spelling of common words and the preferred usage of debatable grammatical forms, as well as which words are capitalized and what punctuation is used. Small publications may not have their own style book but may use that of a larger paper. The Associated Press style book is a good one and is readily available and inexpensive.[1]

Radio and television are two other commonly used media to learn about. Libraries should develop contacts at their local stations with the heads of programming and the persons in charge of news, public service announcements (which you can probably get free), and special departments such as a calendar of events and interview shows. As with newspapers, it is important to know the most convenient times to get in touch with them and the deadlines for the various programs. For radio, you will want to know if the station will accept your scripts and tapes and the number of minutes they prefer public service announcements to run. If the tapes sound amateurish, it is wise to ask if the station will prepare them or—otherwise—to hire a professional. Questions about local TV stations will focus on the visual materials they will accept (e.g., video tapes, 8 and/or 16mm films, slides, photos) and whether black-and-white and/or color is acceptable.

Radio and television writing is a genre of its own. This kind of writing is for listening. Unlike a printed page, radio and television scripts cannot be referred to a second time—if they're not understood when heard the first time. Sentences must be short and uncomplicated and get directly to the point. The rule of thumb: One sentence, one idea. This writing should not be burdened with many figures and statistics, which will only get lost in the shuffle. The writing, basically, should be as close to conversation as possible. To know if the right style has been achieved in a radio or TV announcement, have someone read the script aloud to determine if the main points come across clearly.

The mechanical preparation of copy requires typewriting, double-spacing, and wide margins (40 to 70 spaces for copy, the rest for margins). Paragraphs should not be split between pages. Most abbreviations should be written out, which makes them easier to speak. Exceptions usually include *a.m.* and *p.m.* for morning and afternoon and *Mr., Mrs.,* and *Ms.* Numbers are usually written out in full.

In keeping with normal conversation, contractions are more frequent than in other kinds of writing. It is not only permissible but often desirable to underline particular words and phrases, which helps the broadcaster accent important ideas.

There are many other rules for usage and mechanical preparation of radio and TV scripts, and, again, many books are available. For example, writing for television is generally much more sparse than that for radio, since there is heavy dependence on the picture to tell the story. A source of excellent information is the National Association of Broadcasters, which publishes a number of leaflets with very basic suggestions, including one called *If You Want Air Time*.[2]

Preparing films and video tapes for television requires yet another field of experience and knowledge, and before venturing into it, it would be wise to consult someone on the staff or a volunteer who has formal training. Most library schools now offer courses in this area, and workshops and courses are frequently offered by professional library organizations and colleges. If the library does not have someone trained in video work and there is no highly skilled amateur in the community who will do this work for the library, it is better to stick to simpler forms of publicity or, if funds are available, hire a professional.

Flyers, signs, and posters require still another type of writing, and also skillful graphics. If this kind of material is being prepared for a fund-raising event, the biggest thrust must be to find exactly the right words, the right illustrations, and the right print to put your message across. Generally, the fewer the words, the better the flyer, and the simpler the illustrations, the stronger punch they will have. It is, of course, harder to write a few exact words than a dozen loose ones; so count on taking a lot of time for very little copy. Sometimes it helps to write down as many ideas as you can, until you think the thrust is in the right direction. Then pick out the strong action words that will get your message across.

Some libraries are fortunate to have a part-time graphics artist on the staff, or available to them. If not, a friend of the library or a commercial artist who frequents the library in search of information and pictures for his or her work is often delighted to return the favor by preparing "mechanicals" for the library's printed materials, and sometimes these people are willing to give their services free. Or sometimes a library can get a local company to prepare and pay for a flyer, brochure, or poster. Businesses can frequently use such good works to their tax advantage and may be very glad to help. It is also good public relations for them.

Even if libraries do not have such human resources at their fingertips, it is possible to learn how to prepare an acceptable mechanical. The number of adult education courses and workshops on graphics seems endless, and while a staff member may not consider him/herself an artist, with a T-square, board, graph paper, rubber cement, press-type lettering, commercial illustrations, and a great deal of patience, quality flyers can be produced. The secret is to keep it simple and allow plenty of time to fuse the elements properly. Whatever is sent out is representative of the library; so all its messages should look "finished."

Good, simple graphics and sparse, to-the-point copy are also required for signs, posters, and billboards. And here, two more points must be considered: arrange the widest distribution possible for brochures, flyers, and posters, and post posters and select billboard sites at the busiest spots in town.

Know your audience before you publish a brochure. If the brochure is too expensive and your budget comes from public money, you will have exposed your library to "If they've got enough money to put out that expensive booklet, why do they need money for a new wing? They could have used the money for the building."

Sometimes a combination approach will work. A library can put out a very large, very glossy brochure, to be hand-delivered by trustees-turned-salesmen to persons considered prospective donors of larger-than-average contributions. A condensed, less expensive-looking flyer can go to everyone else, although it contains the same basic points.

The copy for a brochure must be prepared very carefully, especially if your operating budget comes from public sources. The library cannot be put in the position of using public funds to lobby for a new project or service or expansion program. However, the library can present the facts and let the public judge for itself whether or not public money can be spent on the desired project. While it would not be advisable to say "Build a new children's wing," the library can say:

> There has been no increase in the size of the children's wing since 1930 although there are 15,000 more children in the community now than in 1930 and 10,000 new books for children have been added to their room in the library. There is no shelf space to add another new book for children unless a children's book already on the shelf is discarded.

This point, of course, has brought this chapter full cycle—back to publicity as applied to fund raising. The positive attitude has been mentioned, in fact insisted upon, but there are many little ways to make parting with a few dollars for a good library cause more appealing. Most of these ways add up to "human interest."

The cold, impersonal, strictly bookish image that libraries try to live down is often best combated with a light little story full of human interest, instead of a solemn announcement. And it is just as easy— and a lot more fun—to write a human interest story and send it to the media. This can be done during a fund-raising campaign, as well as for any other occasion.

For example, who contributes the first dollar? Is it a child giving a dollar's worth of hard-earned pennies? Or maybe it is $3 or three $100 bills from three generations in a family of library users, or three generations of college alumni in one family. Or perhaps it is the oldest citizen in town, who's been using the library since Year One.

Any of these possibilities would provide not only a story for the newspapers, and a picture too, but an interview for the radio stations and an item for television. And if the child or the oldest citizen in town is accompanied by the family dog, so much the better. Besides children and animals and spritely older citizens, try a little humor in your fund-raising publicity.

Corny? Camp? Probably. But it is also human, and a lot more appealing, to give to a people-place that has a warm glow than to a cold, impersonal institution.

Notes

1. *Associated Press Stylebook*. Associated Press, 50 Rockefeller Plaza, New York, N.Y., 10020. $1.25. Write for latest edition.
2. *If You Want Air Time*. National Association of Broadcasters, 1771 N Street, N.W., Washington, D.C. 20036.

Chapter 6

Fund-Raising Programs

Patricia Senn Breivik
and E. Burr Gibson

Libraries increasingly will need to avail themselves of all reasonably possible avenues of expanding their funding sources. More and more planning considerations will have to be based upon combined funding packages which include money from budget sources, various government grants, foundations, and fund-raising efforts that go directly to individuals and corporations. This chapter will focus on the latter.

Generally speaking, over the years institutions that raise funds by going directly to individuals and corporations have utilized several types of campaigns. The most common types are known as the annual fund, which takes place year after year, usually about the same time of the year, and the capital campaign, which takes place every decade or so and provides a significant infusion of funds for new buildings or additions, and which more recently has been used to provide endowment funds which guarantee a yearly return on investment to sustain the ongoing program. A third type of fund-raising program is more casual in nature and usually consists of attempts to raise money from time to time for a particular program.

Many librarians have had some experience with the more casual approach. Most have a list of needs in their desk drawers, just in case there is some left-over money at the end of the year or in case someone drops in to inquire, "What can I do for you?" Unfortunately, such visitors seldom appear at one's door, and budgets are getting smaller all the time.

Far fewer librarians have had direct experience with capital campaigns and/or annual fund drives. The chart contrasts the elements which characterize these two types of fund-raising endeavors.

Annual Fund and Capital Campaigns

Annual Fund Campaign	*Capital Campaign*
Conducted every year.	Conducted irregularly.
Solicitations are conducted over a brief period each year.	Solicitations often take 2 years or more to complete.
Gifts are paid in cash, or sometimes pledged to be paid within a year.	Gifts are often in form of pledges payable over 3–5 years.
Gifts are usually small, with only 10–12% running $100 or more.	Gifts are large, with relatively few running under $100.
Often 75% of the funds come from 25 percent of the donors.	Often 90–95% of funds will come from 10–15% of donors.
Few solicitations are made on a personal basis, and these are confined to top potential donors.	The great majority of solicitations are made on a personal basis.
Funds are used to pay any portion of the ongoing program.	Funds are almost exclusively used for capital purposes: buildings, equipment, acquisitions, endowments.
Campaign is usually organized and conducted by in-house staff.	Campaign is often organized and conducted by "outside" professional fund-raising firm.
Costs average 15–25%.	Costs average 5–10% (due to size of goal and gifts).

Within all three types of fund-raising programs, a number of activities are essential to success. The planning and public relations activities have been covered in previous chapters; this chapter will deal with four other activities essential to successful fund raising from individuals and corporations:

Identifying and screening potential donors
Setting and meeting quotas
Securing and training volunteers
Building support.

Consideration will then be given to how to approach individuals and corporations for funds.

Identifying and Screening Potential Donors

Once a decision has been made to try to develop a fund-raising program, the first step is to identify potential donors. The following should be considered:

1. Board members and/or a few friends and/or a few foundations
2. Selected library users
3. Longer list of friends gathered over a period of years
4. Prospects selected from the community at large
5. Lists of business houses, organized groups, donors to other civic causes
6. Purchased lists

In identifying your prospects, put anyone on the list who has used your services within recent years or who you feel might be interested for any reason. Board members and development officers can suggest names, and local lists might be made available.

If your library is in a suburban community or small town or city, almost everyone in town can be a prospect, other than families known to have minimum incomes. The list should include businesses as well as individuals. For larger communities and cities, you should consider more selective lists, which might be borrowed, such as membership lists from churches, clubs, school PTAs, etc., as well as lists of donors to other civic projects such as the United Way or the Y's. Appeals can be mailed to these prospects, and donor lists can be built from the returns.

If the area served is more urban, it may be necessary to purchase lists from reputable list brokers—with the understanding that mailings designed to find donors may net very little. The point in "mail prospecting" is to be willing to break even (or a little better) in initial mailings in order to profit substantially in later mailings to your new-found donors. It should be noted that direct-mail fund-raising, using borrowed or purchased lists, is an art, and direct-mail fund-raising experts should be considered.

Since it is best to stay as close to home as possible when approaching corporations and foundations, by far the great majority of entries on the potential donor list will be individuals. The next step is to screen the potential donor list. The primary objective of screening is to sort the list into broad classifications of prospective donors, based on their estimated financial ability.

The steering committee and members of the Friends group can be invited to a meeting for the purpose of reviewing the list. Initially, the decision might be to eliminate some zip code areas as probably not being very productive. Then the community knowledge of those who attend the meeting can start determining how active certain people are and how likely they are to give.

There is a side advantage to this process. The library is getting involvement at a level that is not direct fund raising but is one step removed from it. In the process, the people who help do the screening learn the needs of the library, why a fund-raising campaign is being planned, and the range of needed gifts. Even as they work on the list, all kinds of positive ideas are planted in their minds.

When the screening is completed, the library will know approximately how many prospects are considered capable of making major gifts to the program. Perhaps the knowledge of their ability is so scanty that we know only that a person is considered able to give somewhere between $1,000 and $5,000 over a period of three tax years. Perhaps another person is so well known that it is virtually certain he or she is capable of giving a $25,000, $50,000 or $1 million gift.

If the screening figure gives only a range of one's ability, then the evaluation of the prospects really begins — what can be found out (within reasonable limits) about the prospects which will lead to securing the kind of gifts they are capable of making. What are their ties to the institution, their principal interests (is there a particular objective in the campaign for which they would be enthusiastic), who can best approach them for gifts, and so on? This kind of research can't be conducted for prospects below a certain level, but it should include all prospects who constitute the major gift possibilities.

With this background information, the library begins to make a further refinement of the prospects' evaluation. Members of the steering committee can be asked to make an actual-dollar appraisal of each prospect. For example, a mimeographed list can be distributed and each member of the committee asked to make his/her appraisal of the amount each prospect could and would give if thoroughly informed and excited about the project. Where possible, each member of the committee is asked to rate his or her list separately. After these estimates have been made, the average of the figures can be figured, and in a subsequent meeting with the committee, agreement is made on the "final appraisal" of each prospect.

Setting and Meeting Quotas

Fund raisers have long known the rule of one-third; that is, in every major campaign one-third of the money comes from the top ten gifts, the next third from the next 100 gifts, and the last third comes from everybody else. Once the library's self-analysis and problem definition have determined the amount to be sought, by applying the rule of one-third and some simple arithmetic, one can establish a quota system for the donations which will be sought. This quota system then can be broken down by geographical location, categories of funding sources, or whatever else makes sense in the situation. Or if the top amounts seem too unrealistic, it may call for a reassessment of the overall goal.

Once potential donor lists have been screened and matched against the quota system, the type of approach must be decided, and in this regard the following questions should be helpful.

1. How many solicitors can be recruited (including board members)?
2. How many personal visits can be made? (Each solicitor should be limited to six or seven calls at most.)
3. What prospects—foundations or corporations—should receive typed proposals?
4. For some of the better prospects who can't be seen in person, how many should receive personal letters?
5. What lists should be covered through personalized form letters?
6. What special events might be planned to appeal to identified donors and others?

In planning fund raising strategy, keep in mind that the majority of small institutions that raise money for annual support depend chiefly on a mail campaign, with board members and certain high-potential prospects being seen in person.

Solicitation should begin with those closest to home (board members, officers in the Friends groups, etc.) and those who (from the screening procedure) are known to be the best prospects. Always concentrate first on the highest potential groups of donors. Top prospects may include corporations and foundations which have a record of contributions to the library or particular reasons for giving support.

Solicitation on this level should always be conducted through personal visitations by people who are well acquainted with the library's operations and needs.

It is good practice to have the volunteer solicitors make their own pledges or donations before calling on others. When calling on major prospects, the library director should usually be teamed with either a carefully chosen volunteer, the development officer, or the fund-raising counsel. Sometimes more than one call will be needed to elicit a gift.

Success can be safeguarded in two ways. First, no matter how carefully potential donors are matched with the established quota system, there will be some donations that fall below expectations as well as some that come in at higher-than-anticipated levels. Thus it is wise to have the subquotas add up to more than the publicly stated total goal. Indeed, some fund raisers feel that the total amount projected after the screening process (including projected foundation requests) should equal 250 percent of the campaign goal.[1]

Second, more prospects should be scheduled for contact at each level than the number of gifts required for the level. It has been suggested, for example, that at the top level four or five prospects should be contacted for every needed gift.[2]

Quotas should be well publicized among the volunteers and be reasonable—that is, high enough to make volunteers work hard but low enough so volunteers have a chance of exceeding them. Special care should be taken not only to provide volunteers with sufficient training before they begin their work but frequently to acknowledge their efforts and successes. Such care not only makes for good morale and a successful campaign, it also deepens the understanding and support for the library for years to come.

Securing and Training Volunteers

Fund raisers have long known that there is a direct relationship between the number of workers in a campaign and the amount of money which is raised. It is a good practice not to let any solicitor be responsible for more than six or seven prospects. For others, five is plenty. Since practice has shown the value of having a captain or lieutenant for every five to ten solicitors, it is soon apparent how many volunteers will be needed to ensure the success of the library's campaign. One of the mistakes most often made in recruiting volunteers is to try to make it sound as if nothing much is asked of them. Instead, potential volunteers should be made aware of the truly crucial role they will be playing as solicitors in ensuring the continuance and development of the library's resources and programs to meet specific community needs. The emphasis should always be on the payoff in terms of services to the particular community, not on the fund-raising process. Donated time and effort doesn't supplant the need for money, but it carries its own high value and is obviously necessary to the ultimate success of the campaign.

Where does a library go for its fund-raising volunteers? It goes to the list of potential donors, and it first consults with members of the steering committee and library staff to secure the captains. Then, with this expanded group of committed people, the solicitors are identified and secured.

All the solicitors, whether they are responsible for the top prospects or the smaller ones, need and deserve training. The best approach is to provide each solicitor with an information kit and to provide some opportunity to review its contents in a group situation, which also provides an opportunity for enthusiasm building. The kit should include the following:

1. Question and answer sheet, which highlights information volunteers will need to be able to provide when soliciting their prospects
2. Public relations materials and/or portions of the case statement which can be given to prospects, as well as a copy of any preparatory letter which may have already been sent to the prospects
3. Practical tips on soliciting (see section on what and how to ask)
4. Pledge cards
5. Report envelope
6. Assignment sheets.

There may be any number of prospects who will, for one reason or another, be best assigned to a particular solicitor. This is particularly the case with major prospects, corporations, and foundations. Otherwise, the best approach may be to allow the volunteers to choose among those listed on the potential donor list.

Some volunteers will need more training and encouragement than others, and certainly this phase of the campaign preparation warrants the best possible efforts. If a professional fund-raising counsel is employed, or if the parent institution has a development officer, this should be one of their primary responsibilities.

As referred to elsewhere in this book, care should be taken to give the volunteers all the publicity for their efforts that is seemly. Certainly the campaign-launching meeting is one such opportunity. Additional credit can be given as quotas are reached and at the conclusion of the campaign. There will always be volunteers who drop out, and they must be handled as graciously as possible. On the other hand, it is difficult to fire a volunteer; so if a nonfunctioning volunteer doesn't officially drop out, it is usually better to "work around" the person. Someone else can be appointed under a slightly different title, etc. For those who stick with the campaign and fulfill their obligations, every care should be taken that they feel appreciated and can take pride in "their" accomplishments.

Building Support

A brief word needs to be said at this point about building the support level through fund raising. Once a fund-raising plan has been adopted, it should be followed over a period of three to five years before judging its effectiveness. The fund-raising cost should come down after the first two years or so and then stabilize. There are two main reasons for this.

Obviously, as in any new endeavor, it takes time to develop the procedures and skills that can maximize the return on the library's investment. Secondly, and most importantly, is the fact that the more individuals or corporations get involved with the library, the more they are likely to give to the library, both in terms of their time and their money. People unfamiliar with this basic principle of human nature often worry about asking the same sources for gifts too often for fear people will resent it. The fact is that many agencies find it not only possible but quite beneficial to go back to donors twice a year, or more often, if there is a legitimate case for doing so.

A person who learns more about the library through being a volunteer solicitor for a capital campaign one year, may well run a special event for the library the following year, as well as increasing his/her personal donation. The corporation which donates $100 this year may give $500 or $1,000 within a couple of years. The key to building the support in both cases is that the individuals be made to feel appreciated and be kept informed of the results of their donations.

If funds are raised through the business community, for example, and reports are made to the donors as to how the money has been spent before appeals are sent out the following year, it is very often the case that the gifts from the same companies can be increased because of their increased knowledge of the needs and the feeling that their support is truly appreciated. This fact was underscored in a study made a few years ago by Daniel Yankelovich and sponsored by the Save the Children Foundation on why people give to charity. One of the important findings was that donors want to be told how their money was spent. They feel a moral obligation to help when causes interest them, but they want to know how previous gifts helped get results.[3]

After a few companies have made gifts and shared this information with other companies (which is a common occurrence), it becomes easier to secure gifts from the other companies. In these ways — more knowledge gained because of the gift, and word-of-mouth information — a growth pattern begins to form which can be continued over many, many years. The same thing happens with gifts from individuals, whether solicited by mail or on a personal basis. Each year it is possible to expand the prospect list, as well as the worker organization, and step by step the proceeds grow over the years.

Approaching Individual Donors

How and What to Ask

In each campaign, the potential major givers should be solicited before the general solicitation gets under way. Leadership gifts are obviously crucial to the success of the campaign, based upon the rule of one-third, and they also act as a stimulus to other donors.

One of the hardest things that new solicitors have trouble doing is to ask for a specific amount, but this step is one of the keys to successful fund raising. Through the screening process, a target dona- tion amount should be assigned to each prospective donor who is going to receive a personal visit. In addition to this target amount, it is important that a solicitor know something about the prospect's interests. The target amount, when used correctly with the prospect, is an invaluable tool for the solicitor; if it can be accompanied by a specific project within the campaign objectives that matches the prospective donor's interest, it becomes an even more potent selling tool.

For example, if one is asking a person for a gift of $25,000, it is better to specify the purpose for which the money is requested—such as a reading room in the library—than to ask without specifying a use. In such cases, when the solicitation interview gets to the point that the prospects ask what their share is in the campaign, the solicitors can say, "Will you consider giving the reading room in the new special collections wing?" The prospects immediately want to know how much that will cost and then search for the cost in the list of memorial gift opportunities in the case statement or ask the solicitors to point it out. The prospects do not resent this approach as much as they do a direct request for $25,000.

The target amount is perhaps the most useful and most vital tool, particularly in securing larger or major gifts. The target amount is the suggested amount of a gift a solicitor will ask a prospective contributor to consider giving toward the total goal of the campaign. It is a convincing and a ready answer to a prospect who inquires how much should be given. All people who can give liberally to a cause want to do their full share, but usually aren't interested in giving more than that.

The donors don't know what their share is and have no way of figuring it out. Only those who are conducting the campaign fully realize what those shares are in relation to that of all others who are being asked to give. Furthermore, they have wider knowledge of all the factors determining each one's share. But it takes great care and thought to convey the idea of a fair share to a donor. If it is done too bluntly or forcibly or in any way that suggests dictation or absolute expectancy, donors will resent it. It won't take them long to refuse to make a contribution or to tell solicitors that they can decide this question without help.

Even in dealing with smaller prospects, the target amount and knowledge of their particular interests is very important. Many people prefer to give money for a specific item rather than donate to the library in general, and the case statement should include a list of needed items and projects at varying levels of expense. Where appropriate, there must also be the ability to acknowledge gifts permanently (particularly memorial gifts) through plaques, bookplates, etc., as well as through printed honor rolls. Indeed, "membership" in a Directors' Club and/or other such arbitrary classifications of donations over a certain amount has appeal for a great number of people, despite the fact that such membership seldom carries any direct benefit. All such opportunities related to giving should be well known by the solicitors and, whenever possible, matched with the interests of the prospects.

Besides doing one's home work before calling on a prospect, the following checklist can be useful for solicitors:

1. Make his/her own financial commitment to the library before calling on others.
2. Make appointments with the prospects themselves, taking care not to tell too much over the phone.
3. Be punctual.
4. State the case about the library positively; don't beg.
5. Don't leave the campaign material and pledge card behind for completion; return if needed.
6. Be ready to show the prospect the schedule of required gifts and/or to suggest at what level his/her gift should be. (Some fund raisers suggest asking the prospect to give at the range just above the target amount indicated for him/her.)
7. Give the prospect time to think and make comments.
8. Be ready to give specific examples of what a gift in that amount could do for the library's programs.

9. Have the pledge card ready.
10. Be gracious, whatever the amount.[4]

People are often concerned as to "how aggressive" solicitors should be. Solicitors should be trained to use such phrases as "Is it at all possible that you would be interested in a gift in the range of . . . ?" or "Is it at all possible that you would be interested in funding this particular project for us?" Suggesting specific amounts, letting the prospect know that he is being looked to for a "leadership gift" and/or volunteering information as to some of the leadership gifts which have already been made are well within good fund-raising tactics. What should be avoided is anyone's being solicited by a person who is in a position to be personally threatening to the prospect, for example, who can make giving a condition of employment.

Deferred Giving

There are at least two aspects of fund raising that appear to be somewhat mystical in the eyes of many, including some practitioners. These are seeking grants from foundations and the development of a deferred gifts program. While seeking support from foundations is covered in another chapter of this book, at least a few paragraphs need to be devoted to the possibilities in the deferred gifts area. Although the returns from a deferred giving program may be a few years off, it is a proven fact that interested people will include favorite institutions and causes in their will if it occurs to them to do so at the right time.

We have already cautioned that each fund-raising activity is best developed by starting out with a simple format and becoming more sophisticated as the program grows and prospers. A deferred gifts program lends itself extremely well to this concept. In the beginning the library can, for example, merely publicize the idea of bequests in its newsletter. Articles can describe how valuable bequests would be to the long-term programs carried on by the library and how satisfying it would be to interested persons to assure support to the programs in perpetuity.

Later, more complicated and sophisticated forms of deferred gifts can be developed, if the proper leadership can be found and proper staffing put in place. Some of these more complicated forms of deferred gifts carry the names "annuity trusts," "unitrusts," "pooled income funds," life-insurance gifts, and others. The key feature of each is that the donor (and others) can receive income during their lifetime and receive a tax deduction for the gift.

In terms of the beginning program, what is usually required is:

1. A volunteer committee to promote the program. This committee is best made up of lawyers, trust officers of banks, and others familiar with financial and estate matters. Often, the right kinds of volunteers can be found on the board of the institution.

2. A simple yet attractive brochure or pamphlet, to be used as a basic document. From time to time additional promotional pieces need to be made available. Obviously, the promotion of a deferred gifts program must be very gentle. This is one place where a hard-sell approach is absolutely out of the question.

3. A list of potential prospects. This list should be composed of those who have shown their interest in the library over a period of years, either through the gifts they have made or through volunteer services they have rendered. As is the case for prospective donors to the annual fund program, some names may be found on the library's user file. Generally speaking, the list ought to be comprised of people fifty years and older who are known to have higher-than-average resources. It is easy to be misled in regard to the latter qualification, however, and more attention should be paid to the degree of interest in the library than in the possible eventual size of an estate. Many institutions have received hundreds of thousands of dollars from bequests that ran from a few thousands dollars on up.

4. A plan which, utilizing the committee, promotional material, and prospect list, provides for mailings to the list two or three times a year. All of the mailings should emphasize three things:

a) Everyone should have a will. It is an amazing statistic that as many as 40 percent of people who have died never bothered to draw up a will, resulting in funds being distributed in ways that could hardly be described as satisfactory to the deceased.

b) Those interested in certain community projects and programs ought to seriously consider whether they would like to perpetuate their interest by making provision in their wills. The case should be made in each mailing that, in one way or another, the library has performed a valuable service and that this service can be guaranteed in the future only if continuing support is available.

c) Consideration should be given to the tax aspects of testamentary gifts. Specific provisions in the will can make a substantial difference on the impact of estate taxes, and potential donors should be encouraged to seek the advice of their lawyers and tax people.

It is vitally important in a deferred gifts program to make a commitment to whatever steps are taken over a period of three to five years. Forming a committee and sending only one mailing would be a useless exercise, and stopping a program at the end of two or three mailings would not be much better. Regular reminders, received over a period of time, however, will begin to have impact, and the results will be seen clearly in terms of an increased number of bequests to the library.

Some bequests will be given on an unrestricted basis and can be used either to supplement the annual budget or to develop an endowment fund. Others will carry strings, such as only the income from the principal amount bequeathed can be used. Generally speaking, if the bequest is large and the donor would want to be sure that the family name is perpetuated, it is always well for the institution to suggest this possibility in its promotional literature. A bequest might well be for the purpose of endowing the library director or another key staff position; it might be designated for the purchase of books or specialized equipment, or to sustain an imaginative program of some kind. When deferred gifts of this kind are received, it is important that the library use the name and promote the importance of the funds in as many ways as possible. The use of the funds would always be described in the annual report, and other forms of recognition should be conceived so that others will be encouraged to do the same.

A number of professional firms specialize in deferred giving, and their names can be discovered very easily through inquiries to the American Association of Fund-Raising Counsel, the National Society of Fund Raisers, and other associations and groups in the fund-raising field. These companies will for a set fee suggest the various mailings to be made and will offer guidelines for the establishment of the entire program.

Special Techniques

Ideally, every potential donor would be personally visited, but this is seldom feasible. A number of different approaches can allow a library to reach a greater number of people effectively and/or supplement the contacts it has with prospects who are personally called upon. Two such techniques which have been used in many variations are covered in the two following chapters, that is, direct mail solicitation and special events.

Another such technique is the "phonothon," which has been widely used in college and university campaigns and consists of groups of people telephoning prospective donors after warm-up mailings have set the stage. They can be used in annual support campaigns as well as the general gifts phase of a capital campaign.

Darien Public Library in Connecticut is an example of a library which made good use of a phonothon. The Darien library needed $600,000, and although the people in the community had never given any great substance to the library, they turned out to be very willing to give to the construction of an addition. Approximately $500,000 was raised through individual solicitations, and then, for the public in general, a phonothon was staged.

Some 1,450 people in the community were identified who might be interested in the library or seemed to be interested in everything else. It was called a Celebrity Phon-o-thon, and the volunteers called people and asked if they would support the capital campaign. Ten nights later they had an additional $70,000, and 40 percent of the people who were asked to give money made gifts to erect the library addition.

The basic rule to follow in choosing fund-raising techniques is not to try to reinvent the wheel. Follow tried and true approaches. Steal ideas from others who have been successful. One good example of this principle is the basic "walkathon" idea. There is no reason why one could not benefit a library, and it is amazing how much money can be involved in these events. The National March of Dimes raised $10,000,000 in walkathons.

The same potential exists in "readathons," which would probably work best in a junior high school situation. First, the librarian would have to get permission to go into the classroom and explain what a readathon is and how important the library program is, and then ask the students to sign the slip that says: "I will go around and get pledges from the people in my neighborhood of 10¢, 25¢, 50¢, $1 for every book I read in a certain period of time." In each classroom there can be a progress chart for the number of books. Experience shows that in this program the children start reading on their own, are stimulated, and read much more than otherwise because it is not "required reading" but rather a kind of game. Once the period is over, parents attest to the fact that, to the best of their knowledge, their children have read the books. The children then return, collect the money, and turn it in. The potential is fabulous, and it is a program that ties in beautifully with libraries. Why should other organizations have that opportunity, rather than libraries?

Library memberships or memberships in a friends' group for a set amount or donation can also be considered. Many people are attracted by the idea of a "gift club"; for example, people who give $100 are listed as members in a Century Club or any other designated club.

There may also be a separate club for businesses and corporations that give gifts at the $500 or $1,000 level. These membership lists are available for further solicitations. The library asks for the membership donation at one time of the year and for a gift at another time of the year. The likelihood is that people will not only support both requests but that their amount of support will increase as the library builds on their involvement over the years.

Approaching Corporate Donors

It goes without saying that anyone who owns a business on an individual or family basis is in a position to make a decision on gifts for whatever the personal reasons may be. If there is *personal* interest in the library and concern for its well-being, no rationale has to be prepared for a board of directors. When stockholders are involved, however, the company always needs a strong rationale as to *why* some of the profits of the company should be given away.

Over a period of years, the principle of corporate giving has been well established and upheld by the courts, and it is generally thought that some level of support to community, educational, cultural, and philanthropic organizations and agencies is desirable. The ideal position of those who seek gifts is to provide an important service to the community—one that can be shown to be particularly valuable to the corporation and its executives and employees.

Libraries are in an ideal position to seek gifts on both counts. They serve the entire community in which the corporation is located and, more specifically, serve all those employed by the company. Three points should be stressed in all appeals, whether by personal visit or by letter: (1) how many people use the library and (2) how many might be employees of the companies or (3) of a particular company. Libraries which develop service programs beyond the mere lending of resources have even a better story to tell when seeking gift support.

As with other groups of prospects, solicitation of the business community can be very limited or it can be organized on a very formal and extensive basis. In a similar way, the decision process on making gifts varies greatly from one business to another and from one corporation to another. As a general rule, the smaller the business, the more personal the decision by the owner of the firm. The larger the business, the more likely there is to be an official committee composed of several executive officers who screen the requests for gifts and make recommendations to the board of directors. The very largest corporations set aside money for gift-giving purposes on a regular basis and place it in a company foundation, and the company foundation is professionally managed.

In making approaches to corporations and businesses, their size, then, needs to be kept in mind. For the very smallest businesses, personal contact or a personal letter to the president will suffice. For the very largest companies—those that have foundations—a formal proposal should be prepared, as is the case with any other foundation. In terms of organizational structure and strategy, the simplest approach to the business community consists of letters from the director of the library, addressed to all who might be interested.

Higher on the organizational scale, a better program consists of various members of the library, school, or university foundation board writing to people whom they know personally in the business community and following up with a personal telephone call.

The next-higher approach is to form a corporate and business committee, with members of the board and other volunteers recruited from the business community acting as volunteer solicitors and making calls on a personal basis.

A fourth option would be a combination of any of the previous three. A few prospects could be selected to be seen on a personal basis by members of the board; another group could be selected to receive personal letters from board members; and a third group could be selected to receive letters on a broader basis, either from the director of the library or the chairman of the board.

It is always better to start with a request for dollars, but if a corporation does not seem willing to make a cash gift, it may still be possible to interest it in giving a gift of equipment, materials, or services. Perhaps a local public relations firm will help prepare publicity copy, a paper firm may supply stationery needs, or a manufacturer may supply audiovisual equipment. The dollar values are just as good to the library, and, since the actual cost of a gift may be 40 or 25 percent of its retail value, there are certain advantages to the corporation too. If the fund-raising campaign is getting started on a very modest basis, it might be possible to ask a local business to underwrite an initial donor mailing.

It is usually impossible to start with an ideal fund-raising structure; so the most logical plan is to start simply and, as has been pointed out in other sections of this book, refine the plan and enlarge upon it as each new year is approached.

One other point should be underlined in seeking support from the business community: Persistence pays off. To make *one* appeal to a corporation or business and feel that the job is done is a serious mistake. Follow-up letters should go out; the first about thirty days after the initial appeal has been made and the second one thirty days later. If a business does not respond to the appeal in one year, the appeal should be made again in each of the years that follow, especially to all the large businesses in the community. If a proposal has been submitted to a corporate foundation, after a reasonable time a telephone call should be made to the executive of the foundation and, if possible, a personal visit should be arranged.

Notes

1. Joseph A. Ecclesine, ed., *KRC Handbook of Fund-raising Strategy and Tactics* (Mamaroneck, N.Y.: KRC Books, 1972), p. 58.

2. Harold J. Seymour, *Designs for Fund Raising* (New York: McGraw-Hill, 1966), p. 52.

3. Jerry LeBlanc, "Just What Comprises the 'Charity Market'?" *Boston Globe*, Sept. 5, 1972, p. 14.

4. The checklist is adapted from material in the Ecclesine book, pp. 60–61.

Chapter 7

Direct Mail Solicitation

Herbert G. Howard

Most fund raisers agree that the more personal the approach, the more effective the appeal. Next to actually visiting a prospect in person, writing a letter is the most personal way of asking for support. This, then, is the use of mail: to appeal to the people you cannot actually call on; and the number of people that can be appealed to in this way is limited only by the size of the budget and the size of the community of people potentially interested in the library. The degree of personalization in a letter varies, of course (this will be discussed in more detail below), but mechanical devices are available today which can make a letter seem far more personal than it really is.

Lists: To Whom Does the Library Write?

For any mail appeal to be a success, there must be an identifiable group of potentially interested contributors. In the case of the library, there are many prospective donors, for example, trustees, local and community businesses, "friends," and card holders. There are the library's lists of people who have already contributed general support or in some other way indicated an interest in the library. The latter are the library's best prospects and they should be mailed to first.

In addition, "cold" prospect lists can be purchased from professional firms. They fall into two broad categories. One is, in effect, a list of all the people in a certain geographic area. The library can also compile this itself, working from the phone book or directories, but purchase is usually cheaper. The approach might be useful for a public library which wishes to appeal to everyone in the geographical area, while a technical or scientific library might purchase and use a list of subscribers to a particular scientific publication who live within the library's geographic area.

Copy: What Is Said and How

Composing effective direct mail copy is a very special art which cannot be discussed in full in a chapter this size. Many good books and articles have been written on the subject. Since effective copy is vital to the success of an appeal, a library should consult such sources before it begins to write. It is particularly important to keep in mind the following ideas.

1. Everybody gets a great deal of mail these days, so a letter must capture the reader's attention and interest immediately, that is, with the first words of the first sentence.
2. People give for emotional reasons, so copy must have emotional appeal.
3. The letter should talk mostly about "you" — the donor — not "us" and "we."
4. Letters to previous contributors should include an expression of gratitude for previous support, and tell the readers how the contributions were used.
5. Don't forget to *ask* for the gift (you'd be surprised how many people do!).

Format: Typed, Computer Printer? How Personal?

One of the most important ingredients in a mail appeal is the degree to which the letter is personalized. In fact, the appeal's effectiveness may be in direct proportion to the personalization.

Most personal and most expensive is the individually typed letter, signed in ink. Fortunately, there are various devices on the market today which in effect produce a typewriter's type, and there is also a machine which can reproduce handwritten signatures in pen and ink. These reduce the cost somewhat, and the signing machine can save the time of the chairperson or librarian, but the expense in time, effort, and money is still considerable. However, the typed letter is the most personal, the most effective, and should be used for major donors and prospects.

At the opposite end of the spectrum is the printed letter, totally impersonal, very inexpensive, and the least effective, but appropriate for lists from which you do not expect substantial responses.

The computer letter combines some of the characteristics of both the above, but it is not for everybody. Few people today would confuse a computer letter with an individually typed one, but the former permits a high degree of personalization: inside address, personal salutation, and use in the text of the letter of any information contained in the computer record, such as a reference to the amount of last year's gift. The hitch is that computerization of a file is rather expensive and, in the opinion of most people, is not worth the cost for fewer than 10,000 names.

"Package": What Accompanies the Letter?

Brochure

If you are writing to people thoroughly familiar with your institution, a brochure is probably unnecessary and adds to the cost of the mailing. However, for new prospects, or when introducing a new program, it can tell more of your story than can be put in a letter and can add effectiveness. Brochure copy, like letter copy, should be attention getting, emotion oriented, and concentrate on "you."

Mailing Envelopes

To nearly every layman's astonishment, years of experience have shown that "window envelopes" (which are cheaper) are *as* effective and often *more* effective than standard "closed face" envelopes, except when typewritten letters are used, in which case they are obviously inappropriate.

Reply Device

The easier you make it for prospects to send in a gift, the more likely they are to give one. So be sure to include a reply envelope, preferably a business reply envelope, either printed in such a way that the donor can indicate name, address, and amount of gift, or one that contains a card or slip of paper with the same information. Business reply postage is expensive these days, but many experts continue to feel that returns are better if return postage is guaranteed. Others feel most donors have stamps on hand and rely on them to pay the postage, using a printed phrase such as "Please use your own stamp—every penny counts."

Finally, be sure to code your envelopes or reply cards so you will know to which mailing a donor is responding.

Getting Along with the Postal Service

Postal regulations are subject to change at any time, so a library should consult its local postmaster concerning current postal regulations and services before conducting a mailing, *or* ordering stationery, since postal regulations may affect the size or kind of stationery a library will want and what it wants printed upon it. It is the experience of most people that the post office will always try to be helpful if an effort is made to meet it halfway.

First versus Third Class Mail

First class mail is speedy, professional, and expensive. It is well worthwhile for typed letters, but probably not for the others.

Third class "nonprofit" mail is inexpensive and slower. To mail at this rate, a library must pay a fee, get a special permit from the post office, and deliver the mail to the post office sorted by zip codes. This is appropriate for printed or computer-letter appeals.

"Address Correction Requested"

No list of donors or prospects is much good if it is not up to date, and this service, which the post office can provide, is one of the most important means of keeping your list up to date.

If you put the words "address correction requested" under the return address in the upper left-hand corner of your mailing envelope, the post office will (for a fee) provide you the new address of anyone who has moved or inform you if someone is deceased or has moved and left no forwarding address. This service is well worth the cost, but in making successive mailings to the same list, do not use "address correction requested" for more than whatever length of time it will take for all changes to be returned to the library and entered in its files.

Business Reply Envelopes

Current regulations provide different methods of paying return postage. If a small number of returns is expected, one method will be preferable over another — for when many returns are anticipated Check with the post office to see which is better in specific situations.

Recordkeeping: How Did You Do?

After the mail has gone out and the gifts have come in, the library will want to add up the results and plan mailings for the future. This should be done not just for the overall comparison but mailing list by mailing list, for this will tell you precisely which parts of the program and which mailings are doing the best, and identify any that are not successful.

Staff should separately record the number of pieces mailed, the number of responses, percent response, total dollars, average gift, cost of mailing, and cost per dollar raised for each mailing to each list. For example, if you have a campaign comprised of a major mailing and two follow-ups to major contributors, regular contributors, "friends," noncontributors, library card holders, and a purchased list, a separate code should be attached to the reply envelopes (included with each of the three mailings to each of the five groups) and the results for each of the aforementioned categories should be compiled for each mailing. The crucial question, of course, is cost per dollar raised, which tells whether the library is gaining or losing money, and how much.

One point should be emphasized: A mailing intended to elicit *new* donors is intended to do just that. The mailing to *current* donors is primarily intended to raise money. The cost per dollar raised in a mailing to current donors should be respectably low, but a library should not be concerned if the cost per dollar raised in a mailing intended to elicit new donors approaches the breakeven point. The library has not made money—it may even have lost a little this time —but the library has acquired a few new donors who, most likely, if properly cultivated, will contribute more generously the next year and for many years to come. Indeed, it is more difficult to obtain a new donor than to increase the size of gifts from old donors, but the success of future campaigns depends on adding to the donor list.

Counsel or Not—and a Word of Caution

Direct mail is one of the easiest ways to raise money, and also one of the easiest ways to lose a great deal. It is more than just sending out some letters. It is a service, and if a large program is planned with an adequate budget, professional counsel, recruited after careful checking of credentials, is well worthwhile.

If a library is small, it can succeed in a mail campaign mounted by its own staff or volunteers if sufficient home work is done. Read not only material about direct mail but obtain a good number of direct mail pieces and study them carefully. Above all, start small, realizing that all first attempts are experiments; that most of them succeed, but some fail totally because the market simply is not there; and that even the most successful fund raising may occasionally have unsuccessful mailings.

By starting small, a library risks little if a mailing fails. If it succeeds, the library can repeat the pattern on a larger scale. In this way, the library can maximize its income, while keeping risk at the minimum, and continue expanding until it has reached the limits of its market.

Chapter 8

Special Events

Ellen Barata

Whether a fund-raising event is a one-shot telethon, and informal open house, the first of a series of six concerts, or a one hundredth annual box social, lots of planning will be required; and if the event is to be successful, those who attend should get something out of it—preferably a good time, or, maybe, just an interesting, informative evening.

As for the planning, start early. A library might "luck out" and have great success with an impromptu event, but if the object is a sizable sum of money, the library will need to do a lot of planning well in advance and leave as little as possible to chance. A haphazard affair does not bring in the dollars, and it *can* bring ill will, which will not help to raise funds now or in the future.

A good checklist to follow in planning a fund-raising event is to determine the basics, which will have to include—in news releases about the event—the who-what-why-when-where of the special event.

Why comes first. Just *why* is it necessary to have a special event? Even assuming the library needs money for something which qualifies as a "worthy cause," that is not reason enough to give a special fund-raising event. The question should be: Is a special fund-raising event the best way for the library to get the money it needs for its "worthy cause"? The best way to answer this is by the process of elimination. If the city, or the university, or the board of education, or any other group of persons which might provide the needed money will not do so; if the needed amount is more than you could expect to get from a direct mail campaign; and if federal, foundation, business, or corporation grants will not fill the bill, the special event is your answer.

Next on the checklist is *what*. *What* is the special event to be? It is a good idea to tie the event into the purpose for which you want to raise money. Book sales are "naturals" for libraries, of course, and they may be done with many variations. It may be an annual sale of discards only or perhaps of discards and gifts not needed in the collection. You may include paperbacks, periodicals, records, and cassettes. Or if the library is short of space and/or does not have room to store books for a full year, a monthly book-table sale may be the approach to take.

One large system has a small bookstore and sells discards and gift duplicates all year round. Another library has an annual sale in the auditorium, to run four to six weeks every summer. In the latter case, instead of putting all the books out when the sale opens, the librarian puts out a fresh assortment each Wednesday and Saturday so that buyers return time and again to look over the "new" stock. One library, which usually grosses more than $10,000 from its annual book sale, has been known to make $2,000 from the rare-book auction, which is a special feature of the annual sale, as are the publisher-donated books which are door prizes.

Fund-raising events involving authors are also "naturals" for libraries. There may have been a time when authors seemed to gravitate to metropolitan areas, cultural centers, and publishing hubs, but nowadays authors seem to live almost everywhere. So it is not too hard to find a good speaker among those within traveling distance who will come (perhaps for expenses only) to speak at a luncheon or lecture series in a library. They will be especially willing if they have a new book out or one about to be published, and many times their publishers will be more than willing to persuade authors in the latter category to accept such invitations.

If the objective of the fund raising is to establish a film collection, the library may prefer to arrange a film series, or an art exhibition can be held to raise money for a circulating framed-print collection. A series of plays or a single production is appropriate if an addition with an auditorium is planned, or a fair on the lawn with children's games and pony rides if a children's wing is most needed.

A special fund-raising event must *give* something. It is not enough to *be* a "good cause." The event should provide something worthwhile to those who contribute, for example, books which can be bought, the knowledge or entertainment imparted by a good speaker, the "inside" view of a behind-the-scenes library tour, the pleasure of a concert, the esthetic experience of a fine art exhibition. If the fund-raising event does not promise something along these lines, it will attract only tried-and-true library supporters. (The chances are the latter will back the library with money and moral support if a need is explained and they are asked for a donation; no further inducement is necessary.) So if the event is not planned to offer something, the library might as well save the effort of planning a special event. But if it is *new* money and *new* supporters the library is after, the special event must offer something the *new*comers will want.

Who is the next factor on the checklist. To begin with, *who* is going to be in charge? Will the person in charge be the library director, someone on the staff, a trustee, a "Friend," a leader of the parent-teacher organization, a college alumnus?

Lots of things go into the choice of a chairperson. Usually it's best to have just one—the responsibility is fixed and conflict at the top is likely to be avoided. However, there are people who prefer to work as a team, and some events call for a team. Perhaps a husband-and-wife team is appropriate which will reach toward all groups. Though the age of unisex is upon us, some groups are still more approachable by men and some are more approachable by women. If a fund-raising event is co-chaired by a man and a woman, charges of bias should be nonexistent.

There is always a question of which should come first—appointing the chairperson or deciding what the event shall be. If the event is determined first, care must be taken to avoid the "reluctant" chairperson, who isn't wholeheartedly behind the effort because his or her interest doesn't lie in that direction. On the other hand, if a likely person is approached with "We need to raise money for thus-and-so at the library. Will you be in charge?" care will have to be taken that the project that is eventually selected is appropriate for the library and its needs.

Much has been said elsewhere in this book about leadership. In addition to those suggestions, two matters are of particular concern when seeking the chairperson for a special event. First, it should be someone who has been in the community long enough to know his or her way around and to have contacts without being tied to one group only. Expanding the library's group of supporters is a secondary benefit of a successful fund-raising event, and the chairperson who appoints committee heads from various groups in the community brings not only monetary support but long-range support on a broader base.

Second, the chairperson must be able to work well with almost every kind of person, nor does it do any good to have the best-loved person available if that person lets the whole project get out of hand by being so good natured that he/she never puts a foot down even when it's needed. The chairperson must be able to delegate authority and to get the most out of everyone's help, whether that means giving a little push to the publicity person or holding a flamboyant decorating chairperson to a stringent budget.

There are two other *who*'s to consider besides *who* is in charge. One is *who* is most apt to come? The other is *who* is going to benefit most if the special event is a success? As for the first, what audience are you aiming for specifically? Do you want to appeal to the whole town, to the parents of all the school children in the community, to all the college alumni, or do you want a more limited group?

Again, it is a good idea to match the event to the people who will find the cause of the fund raising to their particular tastes. Members of the local symphony society are more apt to be interested in the fund-raising event to add to a collection of musical scores than the members of the local tennis clubs. Likewise, they are more apt to buy tickets for a concert than to an exhibition by a tennis star. If money is being raised for a young adults' alcove, parents of high school and junior high school students are more apt to be interested than parents of kindergartners. And if it is the university medical library that is to be enlarged, the medical school's alumni should be appealed to more than the graduates of the entire university.

Where will the special event be held? If possible, try to have the special event in the library. A basic ongoing objective should always be to bring more people *into* the library, and an attractive fund-raising event can do this. Getting someone into the library for the first time may be the beginning of a new library user or at least a library appreciator. Moreover, when a fund-raising event is held elsewhere, the library loses some of its association with the event almost by default. The question becomes: If the hit play is presented in the school auditorium, did the school or the library give us this pleasant evening?

That is a natural question, and worth thinking through, before giving up performances before two small audiences in the library's small meeting room in favor of one show for a large audience in the school facility. Among other things, the publicity committee will have to go to extra trouble to get across the point that the play is indeed a library-, not a school-, sponsored event. When facilities are less than ideal, and if the fund raising is aimed at improving or expanding the facilities, there is another good reason to have the event in the library.

A cramped (but good) fund-raising event can make the need very obvious.

Academic libraries may sometimes make exception to holding special events in the library. There may be many visitors in the library on a homecoming weekend, but if bigger crowds are to be found nearer the football field, a library fund-raising event might be better aimed at that crowd and located where the action is—near the playing field. Lots of athletes write books about their sports careers or have such books ghost-written for them. Maybe a sale of these books, with the athlete-authors on hand to autograph them, would go over big with the tail-gate crowd near the stadium.

Sometimes it's possible to hold an event in the library on a day or an evening when the library is not open for usual service. It may be easier, at such a time, to move reading tables and some of the other furniture to accommodate a fund-raising program which could not be done in the library on a busy weekday.

If the event can't be held inside the library, and there are reasons for wanting to go elsewhere, try outdoors on the library grounds, or even in the street if the town will allow it to be blocked off for the affair. A temperate climate is not necessarily a requirement for an outside event on the library grounds. Tents with heaters can be rented. This is usually fairly expensive, but if large enough receipts are anticipated from the event, a tent is worth looking into.

An outdoor fund-raising event raises another question, of course: an alternative site or a "rain date" if the weather is bad. If it is absolutely impossible to move the event indoors, a rain date will have to be set, but this means double planning, and often smaller attendance because people may have other plans for the rain date. Optimists will think positively and expect good weather, but it is a good idea to have rough plans for moving indoors as close to the outdoor site as possible and having a specific indoor area for everything planned for outside.

When is next on the checklist. Select several possible dates and find out what other happenings in the area might offer serious conflicts and cut down your proceeds. The busy days and evenings vary from community to community. Saturdays are usually poor for library programming, and might also be considered poor for fund raising, unless tied to other popular Saturday community events. Sunday afternoons and evenings can sometimes be excellent fund-raising times, depending on the event. Concerts or a lecture series are perhaps most acceptable, or something that includes all ages, since Sunday is a family day. If a particular night is "club night," when every fraternal and special-interest organization in town holds a meeting, it should be avoided.

Sometimes other groups will be meeting or holding special events of their own. If these meetings will attract the same people as the library event, another time should be chosen. However, even a national or popular affair may not offer real conflict if it is not aimed at the same audience the library is seeking.

Indeed, what sometimes appears to be a conflict of events can be a real opportunity. For example, a college or university library should not consider a special college day a conflict with a library fund-raising event. Although a direct mail campaign addressed to scattered alumni may be the most common way to raise money for the college library's needs, homecoming, parents' weekends, and other special awards days can well be the best times for academic libraries to sponsor a special event because of the "built in" crowds that will be attracted to the campus.

This is also the case when there is a town, neighborhood, or area-wide event of which your special event can be a part. One New England community has had an annual Dogwood Festival for at least twenty years. Any number of community groups participate by holding their own fund-raising events at the same time. The festival lasts as many weeks as the dogwood blossoms, and during that time one neighborhood association raises money with a house tour, a school group holds a Saturday fair, and the historical society conducts walking tours. Still other groups hold open houses, auctions, and art shows, and all make money for their own projects. This is a fine situation for a library to enter with its special event.

This brings up another facet of who. Who is going to give the fund-raising event for the library? Is the library going to do it alone or in conjunction with other groups? There are two considerations here. One is similar to selecting a site for the library event on library property or at another location. Just as there is the possibility that an event held elsewhere will not be considered a library event, there is the possibility that an event held in cooperation with another group will be thought of as sponsored by the other group. Much of this attitude will be determined by how much cooperation the outside group is willing to give and how much control the library is able to maintain over the event. In one New England community, for more than ten years, not one group but almost twenty made all the arrangements for an annual book and author luncheon for the city's public library, and yet everyone thought of that event as "the library's" book and author luncheon. It was a splendid example of how community groups can give a library moral and monetary support.

If the library's friends' group is sponsoring your fund raiser, the librarian and staff, and even the governing body, may have much less say as to the kind of special event to be presented and about who is in charge. This depends, of course, on where the lines of authority are drawn and how well the various groups get along. Ideally, relations are good and a fund-raising event, especially a large one, would involve everyone. If an event is held in the library, staff and administration would have a hard time not being involved, at least minimally, and the trustees would be involved as policymakers for any event covering the use of library facilities or funds for the library.

The five *W's—why, what, who, where* and *when*—might all fall within the province of the librarian and staff, but in a large library with active trustees or a friends' group, special events are often the responsibility of the latter groups. In a small library, where most of the arrangements may fall to the library director and staff, there will be dozens of details beyond the five *W's* to consider. Here are just a few:

Arrangements for publicity are extremely important. No matter how good or exciting the event, it matters little unless people *know* about it. Cover all possible media—newspapers, metropolitan dailies with local pages for your area, radio, and television. If it is a really big event, space the news releases throughout the weeks preceding the event. Arrange radio and TV coverage if possible, and persuade the newspaper editors to send photographers. If the policy that covers the library's budget allows, consider paid advertising as well as the free public relations and radio and TV spot announcements which fall into the public service category. As appropriate, other publicity could include strategically placed posters, printed announcements which are mailed to appropriate groups or individuals or checked-out in books, telephone calls to selected individuals (that is, presidents of local service clubs, ministers, fraternity/sorority presidents), or publicity items especially designed for the event. An example of the latter might be stamped balloons that advertise a children's fair and are given to the children who attend story hours.

If your event requires a program, a patron or sponsor list can be included (the patrons will have paid more than the usual ticket price, of course), and perhaps a champagne supper party before or after the event can be arranged at which the patrons can meet the speaker, author, musician, players, or view the art exhibit at a private showing before it is open to the public.

Parking needs must be met. If the library property does not provide for this, arrangements can be made with neighbors or garage owners.

If a large crowd is expected, the police department should be contacted. Local ordinances may require the hiring of special policemen or other requirements. Care must be taken to honor fire department regulations regarding the maximum number of persons allowed in public facilities, and if the event includes the selling or serving of food, there may be state, local, or federal health requirements to be met. Be sure the library's insurance covers any out-of-the-ordinary things that may occur at fund-raising events, such as accidents at a fair (on or off the library grounds).

Special security guards are needed for some events. They may be needed not only when exhibits are open to the public but twenty-four hours a day, as long as valuable books, paintings, or sculpture are the responsibility of the library.

Even if the event is a luncheon or dinner or tea served elsewhere, there will be many details to arrange before the event. Are tips included? Are drinks separate? Will drinks be sold at different prices or at a uniform price? Is there a minimum number of meals for which the library is charged? What is the deadline for reservations? Can seats or tables be reserved? How should the tickets (if any) read to be tax deductible, and how much of the ticket price will be legally tax deductible? And for any event, will there be door prizes, and if so, what legal restrictions apply?

One thing is too easily overlooked in the midst of all the preparations for a special event: keeping the library staff informed. This is more apt to happen in the medium- or large-size library. In the small one, everyone is usually involved in preparations for the event. But in a library of any size, the staff is the group that will field the many questions on arrangements from the public; so it is important to keep the staff informed.

One thing that pays off in good will (as well as dollars) is the personal note to everyone who helps with a special event. Write a short note confirming a committee appointment and saying how pleased the library is for such good help with such an important event. Send another note to say thank you, and include some indication of the success of the event.

Don't overlook the officialdom—get the backing of civic leaders and official blessings and a proclamation (if it is that kind of event) from the local-government officials. Make sure they get invitations. The same applies to officers and key figures of an academic institution or school system, as well as to local or state officials who affect the parent institution. As appropriate, the program may include a word of welcome or brief supportive comments by an official or two.

Consider an occasional "different" event as a fund raiser, such as an excursion to a special library. Such a trip can serve two purposes: it can be interesting in itself and it can suggest programs or services that could be implemented at the sponsoring library, such as a trip to the library to see a selected group of films. Then you can go "behind the scenes" as you exemplify a good film library with programming and lending facilities.

No consideration of special events can be complete without mentioning the long-term value of some special events or "sleepers." In terms of fund raising, a sleeper is any planned program or special event which, although it may barely break even or even lose a little money, is such an entertaining or intellectually rewarding experience that it wins library supporters who respond when later approached through a mail (or other) appeal for funds. *Good* special events, whether immediate money producers or not, are good public relations and excellent fund raisers as well.

It would be possible to fill an entire book with a list of special events for library fund raising. Some are old standbys, like book sales and concert series. And some are fads; Octoberfests are "big" just now—in places where alcoholic beverages do not conflict with library policy, and wine-and-cheese parties and poetry readings are on the rise. The possibilities are endless. The only limitation is a library's imagination.

Chapter 9

Government Funding

Ann E. Prentice

The major public source of income for both the public and the school library is the local tax base, supplemented in many states by state aid allotted on a formula basis. Under current legislation, the public library must obtain its basic level of support from the local tax base, with other sources serving as supplemental. In the case of higher education, primary sources of income vary, depending upon the type of institution—public or private. The public institution is almost entirely state supported while the private academic institution relies heavily upon tuition, investment, and other private sources, with some aid from the state. Other funds from government agencies are considered to be alternative funds, and it is the alternative sources of funding from the various levels of government, federal and state and local, with which this chapter is concerned. These are intended to serve as supplemental to the basic library budget and support of library service and should be approached with that fact firmly in mind.

The major source of alternative funding from government is the federal government, which has been involved in the funding of libraries and has provided resources for their programs for some time. The commitment of different administrations may vary, but since the 1950s there has been continuous support for library service. A unifying effort in the plans for service and the philosophy of service to libraries in the United States grew out of a study conducted by the

National Advisory Commission of Libraries and Information Service in the mid-1960s, from which the report *Libraries at Large¹* resulted. Having outlined the need for a unified approach to information services, the Advisory Commission recommended the establishment of a more permanent commission and the National Commission on Libraries and Information Science was established in 1970. As part of the legislation, a national policy statement was included:

> The Congress hereby affirms that library and information services adequate to meet the needs of the people of the United States are essential to achieve national goals and to utilize more effectively the nation's educational resources and that the Federal Government will cooperate with State and local governments and public and private agencies in assuring optimum provision of such services.²

The National Commission would advise the President and Congress on the implementation of national policy through the use of statements, presentations, and reports and would develop national plans and coordinate activities for information services. The commission developed a framework for information access on a national scale, including the contribution of both producers and disseminators of information. The plan was based on five assumptions—that information is a national resource, that all citizens have an equal right to access, that networking will be achieved through technology, that economic viability of providers of information is essential, and that individual units maintain autonomy. The NCLIS plan for cooperative efforts and planning for all information services is a move in the direction of national planning. The extent of its impact on the direction of federal funding is not certain. Neither is the national plan completely accepted or acceptable to all of the information agencies for which it has developed an overall plan. Its importance here is that it provides a framework for the direction of federal funding for libraries and as a focus for legislation which can be identified as alternative funding.

The National Commission became operational some fifteen years after the advent of substantial federal funding for libraries. The earlier legislation providing funding for school, public, and academic library programs emphasized many of the points later incorporated into the national plan, such as cooperation and the networking concept. Although there now is a national plan, which is seeking acceptance, there is also a body of library-related legislation which does not necessarily conform to the national plan and which predates the

National Commission. When seeking funding sources and the ways in which to assess them, it is necessary to be aware of the effort by NCLIS and other agencies to develop, within the political realities, a set of national priorities for information services. When applying for federal monies for your library, it is essential to be aware of these priorities, to consider the program for which you are applying in relation to national priorities, and to make application for funds with them in mind.

In dealing with federal funding, there is a further definition to consider—the difference between categorical and noncategorical aid. Categorical aid is funding provided under a specific legislative act for a specific purpose. Much federal legislation falls in this category, such as the Library Services and Construction Act, the Elementary and Secondary Education Act, and the Higher Education Act. Each is available from the federal government to serve specific local needs and to support federal priorities. Noncategorical aid usually takes the form of block grants to state and local government which can be spent within minimal guidelines or with no guidelines. This second form of aid is best exemplified by the State and Local Fiscal Assistance Act (PL 92-512), first passed in 1972 and renewed in 1976 for an additional five-year period beginning in 1977. This act, more commonly referred to as revenue sharing, is a noncategorical aid plan in which the federal government distributes funds to state and local governments on the basis of a formula that combines population, tax collections, and categorical income. The use of federal funds in categorical legislation (furthering specific federal priorities on a local level) or noncategorical aid (use of generally unrestricted funds to meet local priorities) is strongly supported on both sides. In the case of library legislation, the two may work against one another. As an example, the growth and development of a national information network has been supported by categorical funding. When noncategorical funds are spent on libraries they usually support local needs, such as buildings, rather than the overall need for free flow of information.

The major noncategorical legislation is revenue sharing. It has distributed, since 1972, approximately $5 billion per year to state and local governments. Under the first revenue-sharing legislation (1972–76), money was to be spent according to a set of priorities outlined by the federal government. The state would receive one-third of the funds and the localities the other two-thirds. These priorities included public safety, environmental protection, public transportation, health, recreation, libraries, social services for the poor and aged, and a miscellaneous priority called financial

administration—or any ordinary and necessary expenditure authorized by law. Money was not to be used in support of education. The
1976 extension of revenue sharing did not include the priority listings, but instead required public hearings prior to expenditure decisions at the local level.

Libraries have not fared well under the noncategorical aid program. They have had to compete at the local level with other priority
areas and library service has not had the political clout at the local
government level that can be brought to bear in support of items such
as public safety or transportation. Possibly with the requirement for
public hearings prior to expenditure decisions, services such as
libraries will be more successful in indicating the need for the right to
a portion of revenue-sharing funds. As a source of funding for the
public library, revenue sharing is of prime importance and the board
and director of the public library must maintain pressure at the local
and state levels to obtain funds to supplement their budgetary requirements. This is done locally in competition with other local
needs, and the library's success here is directly related to its ability to
convince the local government and residents of its need for funds to
maintain the high level of service the community has the right to
expect.

Categorical aid to libraries is the form of most other sources of
federal funding. Program-related legislation applies to all types of
libraries and related public information and education agencies. Programs which are fundable and agencies which are eligible for funding
may change from year to year, as does the appropriation, in support of
the legislation, and it is important to monitor the legislation and be
aware of the current status of those items of particular relevance to a
particular agency. The basic source of information is the annual
Catalog of Federal Domestic Assistance,[3] which includes all funded
legislation currently in effect in the United States and provides
information on its objectives, who may apply, what restrictions exist,
and additional information related to the technicalities of
application.

To maintain a regular update on new legislation and the status of
pending legislation, the best source is your U.S. congressman. This
has a dual purpose in that it keeps the librarian regularly informed
about legislation of importance to the library and its needs and it
keeps the congressman aware of the concern by members of his
district with library-related legislation. Good political channels are
always helpful in requesting funds or supporting specific legislation.
If difficulties arise in preparing requests for federal funding, one
source of assistance is your congressman's local office.

The following review of legislation in support of library and library-related programs is not complete but rather indicative of the wide range of legislation available to the librarian in search of funding. The funding itself is intended to be supplementary and not a replacement of existing funds, and is most often in support of innovative programs. In some instances the funding is tied to existing levels of local support and serves as matching funds or as challenge grants, or it may be a formula grant and thus tied to indexes such as local per capita income. It may be in the form of a project grant for which a specific contract is written in support of a particular program. Many services, particularly information services, are free to qualifying agencies.

Before 1956, funding from the federal government was not a major factor in library service. Due to increasing pressure by library organizations for a federal role in library development and services, the Library Services Act (PL 84-597) was passed in 1956. Before that there were isolated instances of federal support for libraries, but it was minimal and not sustained. The Library Services Act was aimed at strengthening state library agencies and developing regional system plans for libraries. Another thrust of the Library Services Act was to provide funds for upgrading public service in areas unable to afford to improve their own service—rural areas in particular. Passage of the Library Services and Construction Act in 1964 (PL 84-597, as amended) as a continuation of this legislation included service to the urban unserved as well.

In a hearing concerning possible amendments to the LSCA in December 1975, Alphonse Trezza, director of the National Commission on Libraries and Information Science, stated that the federal government should leave basic support for operation and construction to state and local governments and "encourage, support and provide incentive capital for comprehensive informational services in inter-institutional cooperative patterns and to demonstrate these, as well as other related arrangements of new information delivery systems for libraries of all types."[4]

The developing emphasis in terms of LSCA funding is in the extension of services to unserved clienteles and areas for bilingual programs and for materials and staff to support these programs, while Title III supports the continuing effort to develop and maintain cooperative services among libraries. In addition, LSCA monies were initially available on a matching basis for construction. Funds under this legislation were to be approved at the state level by state library agencies. The library construction title of LSCA has had zero funding for several years, and although still on the books, the funding prospects are dim. A better source of building funds is revenue-sharing funds or state-level sources in states which support building programs. Although LSCA is the first place public librarians and public library system personnel look when seeking federal funding for programs, it should not be the only place.

The Higher Education Act (PL 89-329, as amended) supports program efforts intended largely but not exclusively for the support of higher education. Under Title II, funds are available for acquisition of materials both basic and supplemental, for research and demonstration grants in several areas of librarianship, for institutes that provide training for librarians, trustees, and other information personnel. Additional titles of HEA support undergraduate instruction (but not library acquisition) and development grants to set up programs to assist in solving community problems. This act with its various possibilities, although not richly funded, has been important to the development of library programs.

The Elementary and Secondary Education Act (PL 89-10, as amended) remains the major legislation for support of library-related programs in the schools. Funds are available for special projects and resources to prevent students from dropping out of school, for programs to help the handicapped in the schools, for migrant children, for bilingual education, and for programs in ethnic heritage. Funds are also available for resources in support of these programs.

In addition to these three basic pieces of legislation, the federal government provides funding under a wide range of programs which apply to libraries and the services they provide. To some extent, the legislation can be categorized by type of library eligible to apply, but a more functional division is by type of support available. Under this division are three general categories: program development and support, staff support in terms of funds to employ personnel, and information support, which can range from technical information to free loan of films, exhibits, and learning programs. In addition, there is legislation which fits in none of these broad categories, such as legislation dealing with the utilization of surplus property. This legislation enables publicly supported institutions to buy, exchange, or receive as gifts, property and goods no longer needed by the federal government. The range can be from a postal box for use as a book return drop to an entire post office building no longer in service. Although seldom helpful to libraries, legislation also permits the sale of public lands to public agencies at minimal cost.

Much of the program-related legislation is tied in with instructional support programs for particular target groups and is funded through the U.S. Office of Education. These include the Adult Education Act (PL 91-230), which provides support programs in basic education, the Bilingual Education Act (PL 91-230), the Civil Rights and Technical Assistance and Training Act (PL 88-352), the Vocational Education Act (PL 90-576), and Headstart legislation (PL 93-644)— each aimed at dealing with a special educational program area. Each provides funding for program support, which can include books, films, and other informational material needs required to implement the program.

The National Defense Education Act (PL 85-864) provides library facilities and staff support in modern foreign language and critical area studies programs. Legislation in support of education for the handicapped supports research in the area of special needs of this target group, plus the funds for regional resource centers for their educational support. Resources such as captioned films for the deaf and funds to support dissemination of information concerning the handicapped are available. Several acts deal with consumer education programs, and funds are available to develop programs and acquire materials in their support. For development of programs to provide information on energy, the environment, and pollution, several possibilities exist. Also, the Energy Research and Development Administration has for loan and/or distribution support materials such as films, publications, exhibits, and technical information.

Librarians, in planning programs, would be well advised to consider joint submission requests for funding—for example, a joint request with a local environment group when planning an energy program. Although many of these programs may not be related to what a library does, and may not be directly in support of collection or staff development, each does or can have a library element and can enrich the library's programs and resources.

Additional legislation that is helpful to libraries includes the University Community Service–Special Projects legislation (PL 89-329, as amended by PL 92-318), aimed at seeking solutions to national and regional problems related to technological and social changes and environmental pollution and it is suggested for academic libraries that work jointly with campus groups or departments. Right to Read legislation (PL 93-380) supports the objective of increasing the level of functional literacy, and money is available for programs in and by library agencies to achieve this aim. Research and program support is available to medical libraries through the Medical Library Assistance Act (PL 93-353) and various aspects of legislation under the Publlic Health Service. (This listing is only indicative of the possibilities for program and resource support funding for libraries which is available under currently funded categorical legislation.)

Of particular importance to libraries is the National Endowment for the Arts and Humanities (PL 89-209, as amended). Divided into two separate units, each provides project grants in support of specific facets of the arts or humanities, and in some instances their application to specific areas of the country. The artist is the focus of the legislation, but the support vehicle the artist uses in developing a film or teaching or reading his poetry has often been a library.

A second type of legislation that is useful to libraries is that which funds individuals who work in libraries. The basic purpose of these acts is not to help libraries but to give people jobs. Some of these acts are tied to vocational concerns and pay the salaries of people who will learn on-the-job skills and gain experience to fit them for work elsewhere. This can (for example) include specific clerical tasks. Some acts have as their focus jobs to support students so that they may remain in school. Other legislation has as its purpose the funding of jobs for people who live in areas of high unemployment. The Comprehensive Employment and Training Act of 1973 (PL 93-203, as amended) is one of this latter type and is tied to the economic conditions of a locality in terms of the number of jobs funded in that area. In order to employ individuals under CETA legislation, it is necessary to be a public institution. Further, the jobs are allotted to local government, which then assigns them to specific agencies. Library administrators must apply locally to obtain CETA personnel and must be alert to know the number available locally and the number for which the library may fairly ask.

The final type of legislation covers a multiplicity of information and information-related services. Much of this is free or available on loan. Librarians should review the variety of services available and determine those relevant to the library's program, and then request those most pertinent to that program. Nearly every agency provides technical information and statistics on its services. For statistical information, maps, publications, educational programs, and information, the sources are many, and free from the Bureau of Labor Statistics, U.S. Geological Service, Internal Revenue Service, Department of Agriculture, Bureau of the Census, National Bureau of Standards, and National Weather Service—to cite representative examples. The Library of Congress is one of several government-funded agencies which provides free, or at a minimal fee, a range of services including cataloging data distribution, reference services on site, and, as a backup, consultation on preservation of materials (among many others). The Smithsonian Institution provides similar support services from its collection, consultants, and loan items for exhibit. The National Gallery of Art also provides loan materials.

To apply for funding or to request services from any federal source, it is important to review the library's program, determine unmet needs or new directions the library should consider, and then, reviewing existing legislation, determine if funding possibilities are available. Refer to your congressman any questions related to the current status of the bills which are of interest. Determine the projects which meet your needs, and which also appear to be popular with the funding agency, and make application for those funds which are relevant to your community and your library's program.

State Patterns of Funding

State funding for libraries varies in philosophy and application, depending upon the particular state. Because of the impact of LSCA funds aimed at developing state-level plans for library service and at strengthening the state-level library agency, each state has an organized central library agency with a plan for orderly library service within the state. The plans for service incorporate the following elements.

1. Stimulation of local public library support
2. Equalization of opportunity between rich and poor areas
3. Relief of the local tax load
4. Provision for richer public library programs
5. Recognition that state government has a responsibility to support the flow of information.[5]

These plans and implementing agencies vary in the length of time they have been in operation and in the complexity of level of service, but all have the requirements of LSCA legislation as their base lines. Public libraries are the focus of most of the planning, but many state agencies include academic libraries and school libraries within the overall plan.

It is within the library network concepts and within these guidelines that the state-level agency will decide which LSCA requests from individual libraries fit within the state plan and which will be funded. In some instances the state-level agency will suggest that a particular library apply for a grant of money to meet one of these objectives, such as development of a new program in support of a specific need. The state agency is also responsible for the allocation of some other federal categorical aid, and of any noncategorical revenue-sharing money received by the state and used for library service.

In addition to this role, the state agency is responsible for supporting state-level programs which will be of benefit to library services within the state. Much of the legislation is oriented to an entire organization such as the college or the school or the public library. The aid is often in the form of grants-in-aid through public library systems and regional reference systems (as in New York, Illinois, and California), support of district centers which provide supplementary services (as in Pennsylvania and New Jersey), and direct aid to libraries that meet minimal local per capita standards.

Important to the funding possibilities for libraries is money from a state's council on the arts. Each state has such an agency, responsible for the development and funding of programs in the arts. Much of the funding from the National Endowment for the Arts is portioned out to state agencies, and this, plus state-level monies, is the source of the councils' funding. Librarians applying for a council grant have received money to support a variety of programs—collection development in the arts and humanities, when tied to a particular program or artist; funds to support plays, poetry writing, and film development; and subsidies for programs in support of particular arts and artists. Such money is to support the artist and the product rather than the library, but the library often provides the optimum environment for such activity. Some librarians have written proposals independently, while (for example) in other instances joint proposals with artist leagues and local theater groups have been developed.

In some states, such as West Virginia and Massachusetts, legislation provides funding for the establishment of libraries and media centers. With the Massachusetts legislation in particular (Comprehensive Library Media Services Act, 1974), there is an expectation of strong local support and a desirable level of local funding prior to the state's decision to make a contribution.

A further type of state funding is in the area of collection development and staff support. The Massachusetts legislation provides for support of cooperative program development within and among states. Special legislation for collection development is probably the most common form of state-level support. Some states also fund bookmobile services, Mailbook, and services in support of programs for the handicapped and the institutionalized who are in public facilities. External degree programs and independent learning programs are dependent upon local library resources for their existence, as this is an aspect of public education for which some states have accepted responsibility. Connecticut libraries have become involved in counseling, testing, and readers' service programs.

Specific state-level legislation providing categorical funds to libraries is not extensive. Maintaining close contact with your representatives to the state legislation and asking for help in identifying and applying for funds is important here, as it is on the national level. It is also important to keep in touch directly or through the proper channels with the state-level library agency which maintains a close watch on library-related legislation. Here, as on the federal level, funding is political and responsive to the expressed needs of the community, as transmitted to legislators, and library personnel need to play an active role in the development of legislation for libraries in order to have funds made available.

Local Funding

Local government is not often a source for alternative funding. Local funds are used to provide the basic tax support and locally viable project requests should be part of the basic budget request. Possibilities exist, however. If county government is not directly responsible for public library service in the area, libraries within the county have, with some success, requested funding on a per capita basis for each library in the county. Special-purpose funds to develop a regional bibliography, to provide service to county or municipal jails and other public institutions, or to develop an information service for the county or local government itself are possibilities for funding requests. As the concept of regionalization of resources, including information resources, develops, there are more possibilities for local yet multijurisdictional funding.

Bond Issues

A bond issue is the community's commitment of future revenue for current purposes, or, as it has been defined, a loan on the future for long-term projects not fundable in the present. A bond issue is a specific request for a specific purpose, which is submitted to the community for its response through a referendum. For major projects, usually building or renovation, libraries may wish to investigate the possibility of floating a bond issue. For libraries other than public libraries (but those that are publicly supported), the school or academic institution will float the issue and the library would be part of such a project. Library bond issues are largely of interest to the public library.

The need for a new building or addition to an existing building or branch does not appear suddenly but develops over time. As the need develops, library planners keep the community aware of the growing need, so that when a bond issue is proposed it is seen as the reasonable solution to the problem. Emergency situations occur, such as fire or flood, but insurance should cover much of this expense, and in such circumstances there is often an outpouring of community sentiment to assist in restoring service.

Libraries are often not the community's first priority item, and it is essential that the members of the local governing body be kept aware of library needs as they develop. It would be unwise to approach the voters with a recommendation for additional funds if the local governing body were not in accord with the plan. Members of local government reflect their constituents and support as many wishes of those constituents as possible. They are constrained by local priorities, by local and state legislation, and by the budget within which they operate, as well as by the wealth of the community on whose resources they depend for taxes. Members of the local governing body are influenced by the quality of library service, the efficiency of library operations, and the value placed on library service by the community. In addition, the fiscal responsibility of the librarian and board indicates the degree of care with which funds are requested and expended. Local governing officials are also responsive to the economic climate and react in terms of how they believe their constituents would react to the support of a community service beyond an annual budget. "Since the city council must assume responsibility for the city's fiscal situation and since [it] must legally take action on whether or not there should be a bond election, it is obvious that it must be influenced, if not governed by the current financial circumstances."[6] Voters' reaction is affected by these same factors, although their concern may be more narrowly focused on the question of what library service is worth to them and to the community at large, and whether as taxpayers they want to assume the burden of even higher costs of government to pay for additional library service.

Preparing the groundwork for a library bond issue requires careful planning by a group that represents not only the library but encompasses as many community organizations, ideas, and interests as possible so that the proposal will be responsive to the community, and the voters will be informed well ahead of the required referendum. Such issues as location of the library, architectural planning, and cost estimates represent a potential crisis area to members of the community, and each must be resolved to the satisfaction of local government authorities and the majority of the community. Intensive site selection study will have been completed. An architect who can translate the library's present and future program into a functional building, in keeping with the community, will have been retained. Plans and cost figures relating to the site, building, and options (with justification for decisions) will be made available. Using plans and figures developed by library personnel and community input, the library representatives will prepare a proposal for funding which they will present to local officials for their consideration. This usually consists of a thorough review of each aspect of the proposal, with particular attention paid to the cost figures, which will be reviewed and probably revised. They may suggest that all or only part of the funds be raised through a bond issue. Their decision as to whether to support a bond issue and what percentage of needed funds to request is both political and legal. The process of requesting a bond issue is specified in state legislation and is intended to protect local governments by preventing them from borrowing too heavily on future revenues. Limits on the extent of indebtedness are often set so that a domestic public agency (city, town, county, special district) cannot borrow above a specified amount. Local officials will not support a library bond issue they cannot defend on all counts. To be placed on the ballot and to have a chance for success, a bond issue proposal requires the enthusiastic support of local government officials.

Having received the approval of local government, the bond issue is placed before the voters in the form of a referendum for their approval. Usually this is an item on the November ballot, although it is possible to request a special referendum. The decision would be affected by such factors as the probable mood of the voters at a particular time, what other items would be sharing the November ballot, timing in terms of construction, and other library or political considerations (such as the possibility of getting out the vote for a special election). In most states a simple majority is necessary for approval, while in others, such as California, a two-thirds majority is required.

If a bond issue is approved by the voters, local government officials must find a buyer for the bonds. The number of prospective buyers will depend upon the municipality's credit rating and the amount of money available in the economy. If each of the hazards from plan to proposal to referendum to sale of bonds is negotiated successfully, the library has funds to complete its project.

Bond issue referenda are high-risk activities and must be planned with great care. Even then the probability of failure is high. A referendum may fail because inadequate information was available to the voters, because not enough voters were aware of the information, because the timing was wrong, because the voters indicated annoyance over decisions of local officials in an entirely unrelated matter, because the voters were frustrated over the state of the economy, or because of any number of other reasons. Several studies of library bond issue referenda have been conducted, including those by Garrison in Ohio,[7] and studies by Lindahl and Berner of defeated bond issues in Illinois.[8] Each of these studies reported findings similar to those in reviews of school and other bond issues supportive of types of service categorized as "general good"—areas of service whose benefits are widespread, difficult to price, and usually the most difficult to fund.

Both Lindahl and Garrison stressed the importance of knowing who the voters are: their educational level, occupations, median income, and previous voting record. They and other researchers established a relationship between voting behavior and demographic descriptors in that favorable votes on such issues as library support come from the professional and technical groups and those with high educations. Generally favorable votes also come from some low-income groups and blacks. Unfavorable votes come from areas with a preponderance of low-income and industrial workers who are homeowners. With careful preparation at each step, with a large measure of community input in the planning stages, and with an eye to political and economic indicators at the time a bond issue referendum is considered, the chances of success are improved.

For all alternative sources of funding, the chances of receiving requested funds are dependent upon availability of funds, the nature of the request, and the care with which the request is prepared. Success is also dependent upon the appropriateness of the request to a specific source of funding. Some requests might better be made to private foundations or directly to the public. In the development of a building proposal, a combination of alternative sources of funds may be desirable.

When seeking funds, review the library's long-range plan, identify its clientele and their service needs, set objectives and "prioritize" them, and then compare these to the existing library plan. Identify needs which are the library's basic operational needs and incorporate those costs into the basic budget to be submitted to the local funding authority. For additional needs and programs, identify possible sources of funding, incorporate them into the basic budget, request alternative funding from another level of government, and request private or community funding. Only then should special funding be sought for programs which have been identified as necessary to the library's overall program and as relevant to the community.

Notes

1. National Advisory Commission on Libraries and Information Science, *Libraries at Large* (New York: Bowker, 1969).

2. Ibid., p. 3.

3. U.S. Office of Management and Budget, *Catalog of Federal Domestic Assistance* (Washington, D.C.: Government Printing Office, 1976).

4. U.S. Congress, House, Committee on Education and Labor, Subcommittee on Select Education, *A Bill to Amend the Library Services and Construction Act, to Extend the Authorizations of Appropriations Contained in Such Act, and for Other Purposes,* Hearings on H.R. 11233, 94th Cong., 1st sess., 1975, p. 50.

5. Ralph Blasingame, "Critical Analysis of State Aid Formulas," *Library Trends* 19 (October 1970): 252.

6. Alphonse F. Trezza, ed., *Library Buildings: Innovation for Changing Needs,* proceedings of the Library Building Institute (Chicago: ALA, 1972), p. 181.

7. Guy Garrison, "Voting on a Library Bond Issue: Two Elections in Akron, Ohio, 1961 and 1962," *Library Quarterly* 33 (July 1963): 229–41.

8. Ruth Lindahl and William S. Berner, *Financing Public Library Expansion: Case Studies of Three Defeated Bond Issue Referendums* (Urbana: University of Illinois Library Research Center, 1968).

Chapter 10

Lobbying

Alice Ihrig

Innovation, resource sharing, donations, legacies, and bake sales are among the common answers to the question of how to get more money for libraries. Although clearly useful in meeting money problems, in the long run all may harm, rather than help, if they distract attention from the fact that excellent library services cannot be purchased without substantial and secure funding. The public, legislators, trustees, institutional officers, and librarians must understand that libraries live on money and are excellent, adequate, or dreadful in direct relation to the supply of dollars. In short, libraries need to express their needs, to make assertive sounds, and *to lobby* for the means with which to serve the public.

Lobbying is the process of expressing needs to the decision makers. It is one of the ways, in a democracy, that opinions are made known. It is essential for a wide variety of individuals and groups to lobby for a variety of viewpoints so that the legislator, at whatever level, is given (and is faced with) facts and constituent desires.

Lobbying is not threatening—though the reminder of the power of a group with sufficient interest to influence an election is not without influence. Lobbying is not of suspect legality—though organized effort may entail registration of the lobbyist. And lobbying, as ordinarily practiced by the library community, is certainly not akin to the well-publicized abuses of the privilege of working for a piece of legislation. In most localities and states, library representatives are hardly seen as lobbyists but rather as sometime visitors, mobilized for limited and specific action. The once-a-year Library Day in a state capitol may be (and is) a good occasion for library advocates to mix with legislators, but it is hardly the kingpin in a continuous effort to raise the legislative status of libraries.

Where library associations and state agencies have marshaled forces based on a platform carried out over a period of time, legislators have responded.

The following elements are the essence of a successful lobbying effort on behalf of library support.

1. There must be a real need which is defined and expressed in a simple, positive manner.
2. The need must have an appeal for the legislator, who—especially at the local and state level—is interested in what can be done for constituents at home.
3. The need must be attached to a specific solution, such as a single bill or the first step in a legislative program expected to develop over several years.
4. The proposed legislation should have the support of a recognized group, such as the library associations in cooperation.
5. The proposed legislation should have a support network behind it, that is, an organized relay of individuals who will respond to the need for personal, telephone, and written lobbying.
6. The legislation should have strong sponsors. Asking a new legislator is usually foolish; instead, seek the support of leadership.
7. The library community should tool up for the lobbying effort. Having a paid lobbyist is highly desirable. Identifying volunteers with influence is important. Adequate funds for printed material, trips to the capitol, newsletters, telephone, and emergencies must be found.
8. Someone (probably the paid lobbyist) must understand the legislative process so that no mistakes are made, no opportunities missed, and no misinformation given.
9. The lobbying crew should have authority to take a fall-back position. Giving a little may result in the half-loaf that fills out in subsequent years, but the extent of surrender should be calculated in advance.
10. Absolute honesty must be the standard. One question avoided or one fact side-stepped could cause a good program to die for want of credibility.

There are other principles, but these ten comprise the basics of a successful lobbying effort. The library community *must* lobby; the activity is not optional. Patrons need this representation, users and nonusers alike—the benefits of professional acceptance of the role of working for legislation that will result in better services.

On the assumption that library associations are the proper representatives to initiate and support lobbying, a look at the process of lobbying is germane. The lobbying position of the associations will be strongest if based on a platform, that is, a succinct statement of the legislative objectives of the librarians, trustees, and friends in their positions as representatives of the public interest.

The platform should derive from a process. Problems should be brought to the attention of an association committee with the charge of generating recommendations for solutions. The suggestions should be scrutinized by members of the association as well as by friendly legislators and the state library agency, who can react to the practicality of the scheme. Platform statements should be reduced to the succinct-sentence level, conveying a general aspiration. Then the details of a proposed law can be outlined to show how its provisions would achieve the platform statement.

It is well to say at this point that multiple groups should be satisfied with the projected solutions. All library associations and units should be consulted, with due attention to discovering area differences, threats to existing programs, and missed considerations. In return for the opportunity to contribute and comment, cooperating groups should expect to be a part of the lobbying effort. It is important that librarians, regardless of the type of library they represent, be supportive of the platform. The competition for public funds is too fierce for librarians not to present a united front, and solidarity from a variety is an impressive front.

Clearly, there should be reins on the selection of a platform. Someone has to remember that a rash of bills cannot be expected to gain the attention that a few well-chosen issues can attract. Priorities must be given so that the target body is not expected to cope with every idea someone wants to see enacted. A platform which cannot be expressed on one piece of paper is too much. Saving some points for years to come is better than confusing legislators with volume.

Experienced writers of platforms will watch the words carefully. Criteria are short statements, action words, built-in appeal, simplicity, and no limiting detail. The platform will be the printed basis for testimony for recruiting volunteer lobbyists, letters, and conversations. It should be brief and basic and suitable as the general foundation of specific proposals.

Drafting the specifics is important to the success of the lobbying effort. The suggested solution must be practical, somewhat related to current law, and highly supportable with facts. Quantum jumps are rare in library law. New bills are expected to build on the old, though directions may change.

Much library legislation is on the appropriation of funds. The tiny corrective measure which straightens out a quirk in the law is easy to pass. Money is always a problem, even in simply renewing ongoing support.

Getting money for libraries is difficult and will continue to be so, unless the lobbying effort is well organized and soundly based. Lobbying for money takes place at many levels. Staff members lobby for money when they advocate new services. Trustees lobby for money when they face officialdom. Librarians lobby when they develop budgets. Patrons lobby when they make demands or dictate priorities through their use of services. But the three levels of most interest are the local unit of government, the state legislature, and the U.S. Congress.

Local units of government differ across the country in their power over library funding, but in most cases library boards report to some authority and must justify expenditures to some group. If boards are to achieve adequate funding for their libraries, they must lobby at the money source.

Lobbying with controlling units of government is a neglected area. Many libraries try to avoid this contact, hoping that last year's budget will survive the cost-cutting syndrome. Relatively few library trustees and library staffs plan for continuous lobbying, that is, special services to units of government, occasions at which trustees/ staff and elected officials can meet the public presentations of library progress and problems. The extent and type of lobbying at this level is a decision to be made on the basis of risk, probable success, and timing. There are routine relationships which result in supporting the libraries. There is also the probability that cultivating closer relationships by sharing information will result in better understanding and better support.

Lobbying for school or academic libraries is somewhat more complicated, because funds must usually first be secured for education. Once these allocations are made, lobbying efforts are crucial to ensure libraries' receiving their fair share of the pie. Because of this difference, state and national lobbying efforts almost always appear public or large research library oriented.

All libraries, however, ought also to lobby with the public, the ultimate determiner of how much libraries mean in the list of public services. It is lobbying for the future to give the best service possible, to share problems, to ask for help and advice, and to have in mind a list of the people who will help when the library needs it. When funding boards, school boards, and academic officers are faced with enthusiastic support from the public, they are likely to listen more carefully than when librarians speak alone.

While the library associations and the state agencies are lobbying leaders, they must not forget that they propose to speak for many people. Representation from the many is vital to a lobbying effort. The process of lobbying should be founded on a broad base, though it is likely to start with a small group's putting out tentative efforts. The core group of lobbyists—that is, the paid professionals and the volunteers — should require evidence of support from the home front. Lobbying can be lonely work if the lobbyist suspects that no one in the field is doing much to help out—nor can it be successful under such conditions.

The formal network of at-homers who will call and write when motivated is the best technique yet devised for reinforcement of the lobbying in the capitol. That network begins with the most forward and aggressive trustees and librarians, for they are likely to be the ones already endowed with connections and clout. Trustees who have gained board status have influenced someone, and the best librarians have identified with and participated in the community. They are already nourishing the grass-roots approach to lobbying, the one-on-one method.

No legislator — mayor, state representative, or congressman — should feel safe from the approaches of the library community. These persons should expect to see librarians in the audience, to meet trustees in the coffee shop, to sit down with the president of the Friends of the Library. Lay leadership is important too; and the at-home touch lets legislators know that problems are local as well as global, that the constituents have a stake in the action. It is hard for any legislator to avoid equating numbers with desirable actions, and the input of the library community enjoys a good reputation for its soundness when its viewpoints are shared by many. If, for example, the lobbying team includes the local banker, an industrialist, and a farmer, the representative will give them attention.

Lobbying at home is pretty much a matter of insinuation whereby the lobbyist reaches a position where his or her name and face are recognized and opinions listened to and respected. The best lobbyists in home situations are those with a known record of participation in community groups, a history of knowing people, and some knowledge of the problems of the legislator. They are the ones with a "special right" to push for their interests. They have earned a following and are seen by the legislator as a pipeline to the community and reflectors of some of the community's concerns.

What the library association needs to do is include these people in the process, as a network of influence. This means communicating with them by telephone and bulletin, supplying fact sheets and timely information, and checking back for results. Many a bill has passed a state legislature because someone at home reared back and demanded a vote from his or her representative. Labels of "liberal" or "conservative" fall before the strong expression of opinion laid down by a valued constituent.

Moreover, it is not necessary to be of the same political party to come to agreement with a legislator. Elected officials respect members of the other party. Once in office, harmony and cooperation extend to most areas of interest. It is helpful if the library supporter has worked in a party, but is certainly not necessary to make this identification to get the ear of the decision maker. Enthusiasm, buttressed by facts, comes through to a responsible legislator trying to set priorities for his or her own performance. The politician who pleases wins reelection. The cooperation that person has shown with libraries should help, and praise from the library community is justified. Electing people who please the voter is the name of the game. If there is to be good library legislation, there must be approaches to the candidate and the incumbent, the aspirant as well as the veteran. A special-interest group should express its special interest.

While lobbying at home is both essential and effective, lobbying in the capitol is necessary. And this lobbying is best carried on by a professional who is paid. Sometimes library people resist this step, feeling that their lobbying then becomes suspect and unacceptable. This is untrue. Legislators, although happy to hear from constituents, appreciate the economy of time in dealing with a professional, who will supply them with information in their own terms, produce only necessary testimony, and stand by to answer questions.

The professional lobbyist is often a volunteer by descent, that is, a person who has been won over by the job through enjoyment of the process. The professional lobbyist is an orchestration specialist, knowing and sensing when to apply the pressure of numbers, when to initiate the quiet conversation with the expert, and when to bring the process to a head by asking that the bill be called.

Volunteer efforts sometimes flounder because the knowledge of the legislative process is minimal. Those who lobby for libraries should know the score. Well-meaning amateurs, undirected by a pro, can put zeros on the score board.

The Legislative Day–approach has its advocates. Mob scenes can be effective if the tenor is friendly. Demands made over cocktails and dinner *do* have impact, though a one-on-one follow up is good, if only to be sure the legislator caught the ball.

Libraries are also a good subject for the personal campaign platform. A candidate who states his or her love of libraries and intent to aid them has made a positive and acceptable statement to the voters. The platforms of the state and national parties are good places to plant a library support sentence, though far less likely to have impact than the simple cards presented by a local campaigner. Library lobbyists ought to try for prominence in both situations.

It should be understood by all concerned in the expression of preferences and positions through lobbying that there is a contest going on. Persuasion is based on being able to set forth a real need, justify a request, and put a program in perspective. When competing for the dollar, lobbyists need to marshal numbers, not only the believable explanation of why money is needed by the numbers of home folk who will benefit from the program. Home-front impact is the best argument, and libraries need to learn to make it. Will funds create jobs, provide services to local people, result in more effective programs? The answers are better arguments than the simplicity that libraries perform good services. The sales pitch had better be good. Libraries had better be able to sell their services. The *concept* of a library goes only so far as an appealing idea. It must be brought up to date and made appetizing.

Lobbying is part of the system, not an adjunct or afterthought. At its best, lobbying is communication that results in progress for a service the library community and a large share of the public regard as necessary for getting ahead and being part of the citizenry of the United States. If libraries really are needed and necessary, if they offer essential services and opportunities, they deserve a better station in life. Library advocates are needed. Lobbying must be done and libraries must be promoted if the profession and its supporting officers and public are to be considered as functioning on behalf of the general public.

Chapter 11

Foundation Funding

Thomas R. Buckman
and Sherry E. Goldstein

In 1960 the Foundation Center began to record and publish brief descriptions of grants of $10,000 or more, based on information supplied by cooperating foundations. Through the years the listings have been representative of the giving of nearly all the larger foundations, and the number of foundations whose grants are reported has been increasing. Many grants to libraries were included. The existing data, if put into machine-readable form, we believed, might yield interesting results. Accordingly, in 1972, with the encouragement of Frederick Burkhardt, chairman of the National Commission on Libraries and Information Science, the center began an analysis of foundation grants to libraries and related activities, based on a computerized file of grant information which covered the thirteen-year period 1960–72. The file includes every grant made for library activities that appeared during these years in *The Foundation Grants Index*, the Foundation Center's bimonthly report of recent grants.

There is a total of 1,820 grants from 508 foundations in the file, and recipient organizations in forty-seven states and forty-seven countries are represented. The total value of the grants is over $202 million for this thirteen-year period. Although it is not exhaustive in its coverage, the data bank is representative of private philanthropy in the library field, especially among the larger foundations. Moreover, its scope is broad: The list of recipients includes not only libraries but a number of institutions engaged in research, maintaining special collections, or offering a variety of information services. Our preliminary analysis of the data leads us to some generally valid observations.

First of all, the total amount given for libraries and related activities—slightly more than $202 million—is larger than expected.On the other hand, the total amount of federal grants appropriated for libraries during the period 1957–72 was about $1.3 billion, according to the American Library Association. Thus foundation support was hardly negligible, but amounted to less than one-sixth of the funds from federal sources. Many of the foundation grants were for special purposes, and not open to general application; for example they were limited to certain localities or had other qualifications attached to them. Federal grants were necessarily administered on a broad, egalitarian basis.

On the average, foundations gave about $15 million a year for libraries, which is about 1 percent of total foundation giving for all purposes for a given year. If total foundation giving for "education" (broadly defined) is used as a base, all gifts to libraries amount to about 2 percent of the total.

It is encouraging to note that there is a fairly steady upward curve with respect to the number of grants to libraries within the United States from 1960 through 1972. In the early '60s there were fewer than 100 grants each year. In 1964 the number was 143, and the highest numbers were reached in 1971 (205) and 1972 (187).

Most of the domestic grants were relatively small; about 1,200 were in the amount of $100,000 or less and 912 were in the $10,000 to $50,000 range. However, there was a middle spectrum of 345 grants which ranged from $100,000 to $500,000 each. Sixty-six grants were about a half million dollars, and of this number only 23 were over $1 million each. The maximum grant was $10 million.

The six largest donors to libraries were, in this order, the Council on Library Resources (132 grants), the Joseph and Helen Regenstein Foundation (1), the Kresge Foundation (87), the Max C. Fleischmann Foundation (36), the El Pomar Foundation (4), and the Ford Foundation (40). The Rockefeller Foundation ranked 14th with 24 grants, and the Carnegie Corporation 19th with 17 grants. The earlier major contributors to libraries—Carnegie and Rockefeller—had become less important in the magnitude of their giving, and many other foundations had entered the field. For example, some that gave more dollars than either of these were the Moody Foundation and the Andrew W. Mellon Foundation.

Of the top 50 domestic grant recipients, all but 11 were college, university, or research libraries. Only seven were public libraries and three were library associations. The American Library Association received the fourth largest sum of money in the list of 50—about $3.6 million, representing 43 grants; the Association of Research Libraries received ten grants, totaling about $1.1 million; and the Association of College and Research Libraries two grants, amounting to $650,000.

Twenty-four states received over a million dollars each for library purposes, with New York again at the head of the list with about $21.6 million, and New Hampshire ranking 24th with $1.4 million.

An analysis of 1,145 grants, identified by type of library, confirmed that college and university libraries are generally the recipients of foundation money, with 569 grants totaling $66.6 million, followed by special and nonuniversity research libraries (162 grants, $39.5 million). Public libraries received 256 grants with a total value of $24.6 million. Others were medical libraries (62 grants, $9 million), rare-book libraries (41 grants, $4.6 million), elementary and secondary school libraries (25 grants, $1.6 million), law libraries (27 grants, $1.1 million), and agricultural libraries (3 grants, $492,800).

Somewhat more than one-third of the total number of domestic grants recorded was identified by the type of library activity given in the grant descriptions supplied by the foundations. In an analysis of these grants, buildings and equipment emerged as the leading category (252 grants, $33.1 million), acquisition of library material ranked second (136 grants, $13.2 million), and endowment funds third (22 grants, $4.3 million). Computerization was fourth (28 grants, $2.6 million), and cataloging received about the same amount, distributed among 56 grants. Undergraduate programs received four grants with a value of $1.8 million. Circulation and reference services were awarded 17 grants totaling $1.3 million. Grants relating to microfilm were in the eighth place, with 21 awards amounting to about $805,000. Bibliographical projects attracted nearly $609,000, and in tenth place was library education (8 grants, $393,000).

Foundation attitudes toward library funding are affected by the characteristics of the foundation and its program, and by community views of the value of libraries. Some of the internal characteristics are asset size, program interest, scope, and size of staff. Large national foundations wish their dollars to achieve the maximum effect toward the solution of basic problems or essential support of organizations of the "national resource" type. Their capability of giving is great but they are highly selective in their grant-making and thorough in their evaluation of proposals, especially if they employ professional staff. Trustees and staffs of foundations may share in the

Two Hypothetical Foundations and Their Probable Attitudes toward Giving to Libraries

Characteristics	Program Interests	Types of Library Grants	Size of Library Grants	Attitude	Application Procedure
A. Assets: $25 million and above (184) Staff: From very large (e.g., Ford) to zero (affairs handled by a trustee or attorney) Annual report: Most publish a report	National and regional	National or international solutions to library problems Operating support for national resource collections Buildings Library support as part of mission-oriented program	$25,000–$50,000 and in some cases up to several million dollars	Skeptical about library grants in many cases. Proposal must seek solutions to basic problems employ innovative methods, or improve established programs of major importance	Generally a more formal style of application, followed by objective staff evaluation
B. Assets: $1 million to under $5 (1699) Staff: Usually no full-time staff Annual report: Few publish; chief source of information is 990PF and AR	Local	Book purchase Equipment purchase General operating Small special projects	$5,000–$15,000 and in some cases up to $50,000	Sympathetic to day-to-day operational needs if they contribute to community requirements	Well-conceived but less formal application; decision-making more personal and less systematic

popular skepticism of libraries as effective modern means of dis-
seminating information, but others may be equally convinced of the
educational and cultural worth of libraries, especially in local communities. Locally oriented foundations also wish to place their money
where it will do the most good, but they are generally less insistent on
new ways of doing things which will serve as models elsewhere.
Foundations are highly individualistic and it is therefore difficult to
generalize about them. Nonetheless, our hypothetical table has some
validity and should help to make some of the differences clear between "large" and small" foundations, and what kind of library funding might be expected from them.

The Foundation Center

The Foundation Center is an independent, nonprofit organization that gathers and disseminates factual information on philanthropic foundations. One of the center's main purposes is to serve as a
useful resource for organizations and individuals interested in securing funds from foundations. Toward this aim the center has always
offered free access to foundation information to anyone who visits the
New York and Washington, D.C., libraries or any of the 74 cooperating collections throughout the country. The librarians in New York
and Washington assist over 18,000 visitors annually, including representatives from the larger established institutions as well as
neophyte fund raisers from grass-roots organizations.

Publications and Services

The center also fulfills its obligation to serve the public by preparing printed and microfiche publications that cover foundation
information in its many diverse forms. The center's oldest and best-
known publication is the *Foundation Directory,* often referred to as
the unofficial bible of the foundation field. Now in its sixth edition,
the *Foundation Directory* includes descriptive and financial data on
2,818 foundations in the United States that have assets of $1 million
or more and/or give at least $100,000 annually. Four indices provide
ready access to fields of interest, state and city locations, foundation
personnel, and foundation names.

For information on more than 21,000 foundations, including the
smaller foundations not covered in the *Foundation Directory, The
National Data Book, 1974–1976* should be consulted. Arranged in two
volumes, the *Data Book* provides alphabetical and geographical ac-

cess to brief entries that include foundation addresses, principal officer, total assets and grants, and indications of which foundations publish annual reports.

The Foundation Grants Index, in its bimonthly and annual cumulations, is equally an essential foundation reference tool. The 1976 annual volume details over 12,000 grants of $5,000 and over awarded by 310 foundations, with a total value of $753 million. The usability of this volume is fostered by its multi-index approach, providing access by keyword, broad subject, foundation name, recipient name and geographic location. A bimonthly version of the *Index* is published in the philanthropic journal *Foundation News.* Another resource that the researcher will find useful in a subject search of foundation funding patterns is *COMSEARCH Printouts.* Computer printouts in 54 broad subject areas list the grants recorded in one year by more than 300 major U.S. foundations. The 1976 *COMSEARCH Printout* for libraries lists 394 foundation grants to libraries, information centers, and learning resource centers recorded in 1976 Printouts are available in paper or microfiche formats.

The center's subscription loose-leaf service introduces a new concept in philanthropic publishing. *Foundation Center Source Book Profiles* provides analytical profiles of more than 500 foundations whose annual giving is at least $200,000 and are not restricted programmatically to strictly local giving. Subscribers receive profiles on a monthly basis. Each profile includes an in-depth analysis of the foundation's grant-making patterns as well as detailed financial, background, and application information.

For individuals seeking funds, *Foundation Grants to Individuals* provides information on the programs of more than 1,000 foundations that have made grants to students, artists, scholars, foreign individuals, minorities, musicians, scientists, and writers.

The versatility of these publications offers grant seekers the opportunity to secure just the type of foundation information they need, provided they know how to use these materials effectively. It was for just this reason that the center published *About Foundations: How to Get the Facts You Need to Get a Grant.* In this guide the grant seeker is taken by the hand, in a methodical step-by-step approach, and is shown the not-so-magical elements involved in securing information from the center's publications and other resources housed within our libraries. All of the above publications are available to the public for free consultation at our libraries in New York and Washington, D.C., and at our 74 cooperating collections.

The center also distributes one to five copies of the following proposal writing leaflets free of charge:

Jacquette, F. Lee, and Barbara L. Jacquette. *What Makes a Good Proposal?*

Mayer, Robert A. *What Will a Foundation Look for When You Submit a Grant Proposal?*

Further information on the Foundation Center can be found in the center's annual report and publication brochure, which are available by writing to the Foundation Center, 888 Seventh Avenue, New York, N.Y. 10019.

Computerized Files of the Foundation Center

At present, the Foundation Center maintains three data banks: the Foundation Directory Data Bank, the Foundation Grants Data Bank, and the Foundation Center National Data Bank.

The Foundation Directory Data Bank contains complete entries for the 2,818 large foundations which are listed in the *Directory*, which is continually updated by our staff. This is an excellent file for generating statistical information on the foundation field. It can also be searched by using one or more of the 36 data fields contained within the entry for each foundation.

The Foundation Grants Data Bank generates the bimonthly and annual cumulations of *The Foundation Grants Index* as well as *COMSEARCH Printouts*. It contains the grant records of approximately 500 major foundations from 1973 to the present. This is an excellent file for subject searches of foundation grants related to your particular field of interest. Both the Foundation Directory Data Bank and the Foundation Grants Data Bank are available for interactive online searching to private foundations, Foundation Center associates, and to subscribers of the Lockheed Dialog System.

The Foundation Center National Data Bank contains brief factual and fiscal profiles on virtually all private foundations, more than 26,000. This file generated the *Foundation Center National Data Book, 1974–1976* and is primarily used for geographic searches of foundations in a particular state, city, or zip code area. Data fields include foundation name, address, principal officer, total assets, and total grants. The data bank is available for searching to foundations and Associates of the Center.

The center offers an "associates program" to individuals or organizations that need frequent access to customized foundation information. For an annual fee, associates gain access to mail and telephone reference and photocopy, computer, and library research services. At present, over 900 organizations, representing all fields of interest, have joined this program.

Sources of Information

For its publications and services, the center relies on three primary sources of information on private foundations: annual reports, information obtained directly from foundations, and Internal Revenue Service forms 990PF and 990AR. Material which is solicited directly from foundations and that which appears in separately published reports provides the center with the most current, up-to-date information on foundations. Unfortunately, only a small percentage of all foundations publishes annual reports or reports directly to the center. Unlike the library field, most foundations do not see themselves as belonging to a larger universe of organizations which have common interests and goals that can be fostered by communication among members. They prefer to remain in the woodwork, visible only to those who take the time and initiative to seek them out, using the information available in the public record.

It is for this reason that the center must rely heavily on the information contained within IRS forms 990PF and 990AR. These are the information returns that all foundations are required to file with the IRS each year. The bulk of these returns are filed on May 15 of each year. The Foundation Center currently receives these returns from the IRS after they are processed and microfilmed. The IRS has made some advances in reducing the time lag between receipt and distribution of the information returns, but progress is slow as IRS priorities lie in the enforcement of the tax laws rather than in provision of information. The center maintains continuing dialog with the IRS in an effort to improve this information environment, but we realize that it may be several years before optimum conditions exist.

Types of Foundations and Their Characteristics

The Foundation Center defines a foundation as a nongovernmental, nonprofit organization, with funds and program managed by its own trustees or directors, and established to maintain or aid social, educational, charitable, religious, or other activities that serve the common welfare, primarily through making grants.

Charitable trusts are included. Excluded are organizations which bear the name "foundation" but whose primary purposes are other than awarding grants—for example, making general appeals to the public for funds, acting as trade associations for industrial or other special groups, aiding solely (by charter restriction) one or several named institutions, or functioning as endowments for special purposes within colleges, churches, or other organizations under the governance of the trustees of the parent institution.[1]

There are more than 26,000 organizations in the United States which fit the above definition of a grant-making foundation, over 2,800 of which have assets of $1 million or more and are included in the *Foundation Directory*. Although they amount to only a small percentage of the total foundation universe, they represent 90 percent of the assets of all foundations and 80 percent of all foundation giving. Foundation wealth is concentrated in the East, with foundations in New York, New Jersey, and Pennsylvania awarding over 50 percent of all foundation grants. It should be noted, however, that a sizable portion is distributed to organizations in other states.

While all foundations possess common attributes, they differ in significant aspects and have traditionally been grouped in broad categories, defined by one or more of the following characteristics: source of endowment, recipient population, size or operational structure.[2] The following categories[3] overlap in function, and therefore some foundations may fit into more than one category.

Private Grant-Making Foundations

Definition: A fund or endowment designated by the Internal Revenue Service as a private foundation under the tax law, whose primary function is the making of grants.

Special rules for private foundations were added to the Internal Revenue Code in 1969 which limit allowable tax deductions for gifts to them, particularly gifts of appreciated property, and which impose a 4 percent excise tax on net investment income and complex regulations regarding administration and grant making, including an annual payout requirement defined as the greater of "adjusted net income" or a variable percent of the market value of investment assets ("minimum investment return"). The variable percentage was eliminated by the Tax Reform Act of 1976 and was fixed at 5 percent.

Many organizations whose primary purpose is other than the making of grants are designated by the service as private foundations because they do not meet other tests for exemption.

Community Foundations

In general charitable purpose, a community foundation is much like many private foundations. However, it has special characteristics. Most community foundations are classified by the Internal Revenue Service not as private foundations but as "public charities," as are churches, schools and colleges, hospitals, and certain other organizations. Their funds are derived from many donors rather than a single source, as is usually the case with private foundations. Grant programs almost always are directed toward the immediate locality or region. The governing board is broadly representative of the community it serves. The exemption from the special rules affecting private foundations make tax-deductible gifts to community foundations subject to fewer limitations and free them from the 4 percent excise tax and a variety of regulations applicable to private foundations. There are more than 220 community foundations in the United States. Their assets exceed $1 billion and their grants in 1975 totaled more than $70 million.

Private Operating Foundations

Definition: A fund or endowment designated by the Internal Revenue Service as a private foundation under the tax law, whose primary purpose is to operate programs determined by its governing body. Some grants may be made but the sum is generally small, relative to the funds used for programs. Approximately 5 percent of the private foundation universe is composed of private operating foundations.

Company-sponsored Foundations

Definition: A private foundation under the tax law, deriving its funds from a profit-making company or corporation but independently constituted, whose purpose is to make grants, usually on a broad basis. There are about 1,800 company-sponsored foundations and they account for about 6 percent of U.S. foundation assets. Company-sponsored foundations should be distinguished from corporate-giving programs which are administrated within the corporation. The latter generally make grants for limited purposes closely associated with the interests of the corporation, although this is not always the case. The two types of giving are often coordinated under a general policy. In other cases, a private foundation, bearing a name associated with a corporation, may have few if any ties with the original source of funds. Company-sponsored foundations are included in Foundation Center publications. Corporate giving programs are not.

General or Special-Purpose Foundations

These are terms which reflect the type of giving or the program limitations of the foundation. Some foundations may give grants only to individuals for research in chemistry or for buildings. Many large foundations, on the other hand, support a wide variety of projects in the arts, sciences, and community affairs. Foundations may change program focus from time to time, and even if committed to certain program areas, may make exceptional grants occasionally. While the larger foundations are usually less restrictive as to their grant purposes, you will find both general and special-purpose foundations at every asset level.

Independent Foundations

There are more than 24,000 independent foundations that receive their funds from a single person, a family, or a few individuals. Many of these, especially those that are small, function under the voluntary direction of family members, and such foundations are commonly known as "family foundations." However, others which may bear a family name, such as the Rockefeller Foundation, have independent boards of trustees and are managed by a professional staff.

How to Do Foundation Research

Before we explore the fine points in doing your own foundation research, it is wise to consider the private foundation's place in the total philanthropic picture. Although foundations granted over $2 billion in 1974, this accounts for only a little over 8 percent of all philanthropic giving[4] and only a small fraction of a percent when compared to government funding in the same areas. Based on grants reported in *The Foundations Grants Index*, only 1.4 percent of all foundation giving was awarded to libraries in 1974 and less than 1 percent in 1975. With only approximately $30 billion in assets and over 28,000 deserving libraries in the United States, foundations are necessarily limited as to what they can accomplish and traditionally have been selective in awarding grants. Grant seekers should be aware of these limitations in funding capabilities when seeking funds from foundations.

Now it is time to get down to the business of finding out how you, as the grant seeker for your library, can make the most effective use of available foundation information. The publication *About Founda-tions* is an excellent tool which pulls together material on the re-sources needed to secure foundation information in a simple, straightforward approach. The author provides the three most com-mon information needs of the grant seeker: finding information on a particular foundation you have in mind, finding which foundations might be interested in a particular project or subject area, and finding which foundations might be sources for funding in your geographic location.[5] The following examples will provide the grant seeker with insight into these approaches to foundation information.

Researching Foundations by Name

Suppose you already know the name of a foundation about which you want more information. You might start your search by checking the *Foundation Directory.* If your foundation is among the over 2,800 listed, you will be able to find descriptive and financial data, includ-ing the foundation's address, officers, purpose and activities, total assets, total grants, and high and low grant amounts. Telephone numbers and application information are also included for many foundations. The information obtained from the *Directory* is just a starting point, but it is useful in helping you determine whether you desire to pursue a given foundation further. For example, if the "purpose and activities" states that the foundation is restricted by its charter to giving in California and your library is in New Jersey, you can stop your search at this point. On the other hand, if the founda-tion's interests match yours, you can proceed to the next step.

If, by checking the *Directory* entry, you find that the foundation about which you are seeking information is one of the large founda-tions, awarding annual grants totaling at least $200,000, you should see if it is in *The Foundation Center Source Book Profiles.* Assuming your foundation is covered, you will find an authoritative, up-to-date profile on it, including a detailed analysis of the foundation's latest grants, information on the foundation's programs, policies, and appplication procedures, and a list of sample grants for the current year. The grant seeker is advised to study this information carefully, as it is the most comprehensive information available on those foun-dations included.

If your foundation is not among the 500 foundations in *Source Book Profiles,* your next step would be to see if the foundation pub-lishes an annual report. Unfortunately, only about 450 foundations publish such a report, but for those that do, it is usually the most important document a grant seeker can find. Reports generally include information on officers, programs, policies, and application procedures, assets, and a complete list of grants. You can find out if a foundation publishes a report by checking its entry in the *Foundation Directory* or the *Foundation Center National Data Book*.

If you do not find an annual report for the foundation about which you are seeking information, you will have to go one step further. For the majority of foundations that do not publish annual reports, IRS forms 990PF and 990AR offer the grant seeker the only other major resource for securing information on private foundations. On these returns you will find detailed financial statements, a complete list of grants awarded and approved for future payment, and the foundation's address and officers. All foundations are required to file forms 990PF and 990AR with the IRS each year. After they have been processed, the IRS microfilms the returns and mounts them on conventional tabular cards called "aperture cards." Complete sets of aperture cards for foundations in all states are available for consultation at the center's New York and Washington, D.C., libraries, as well as at our national collection in Chicago. Cooperating collections have aperture cards for foundations in their own state or geographic region.

Users of the center's New York and Washington, D.C., libraries can also gain access to information leaflets, periodic reports, newsletters, and news releases for foundations which distribute them. These resources usually provide up-to-date data on foundation programs, changes in officers, and announcements of individual grants. If you do not have access to our libraries, you may wish to contact the foundation in question to ask if it distributes such literature. The center also subscribes to a clipping service of daily newspaper and journal articles on foundations, gleaned from hundreds of sources throughout the country. These clippings are filed by foundation name and should be consulted by the researcher for the most current news on foundations.

The steps you follow in researching individual foundations will vary, depending on how much you know about a foundation and the information available. Once all the appropriate information sources have been thoroughly researched, grant seekers can be sure that they have completed their home work.

Researching Foundations by Subject

Another common situation is that of the grant seeker who is looking for funds for a specific project and wants to know which foundations are potential funding sources. Unlike government agencies, lists of available grants cannot be secured from foundations. It is only by looking at what a foundation has funded in the past, along with its statement of purpose, that one can deduce what it might fund in the future. The Foundation Grants Data Bank produces *The Foundation Grants Index* in its bimonthly and annual cumulations, as well as *COMSEARCH Printouts* in 54 broad subject categories. Each publication provides the grant seeker with the grant patterns of several hundred foundations annually.

Suppose you were looking for funding for the expansion of an Afro-American collection within the library of a Southern college. Your first step might be to look in the key-word index of the annual *Foundation Grants Index* under the terms "library (college)" and "Afro-American." You would find several listings for each term, three of which combine the two terms. Upon checking these terms, you would find the grant records of the Southern Education Foundation, Field Foundation of Illinois, and Committee of the Permanent Charity Fund, each of which had given one grant for an Afro-American collection within a college library. Since your college is in the South, you can immediately see that Southern Education Foundation might be a more likely source of support than the other two foundations. You should reserve your judgments, however, until each foundation has been researched further.

Next, you might use the *Grants Index* recipient index to look up the names of other colleges in the South, similar to your own, that you know have received foundation grants. Your assumption is that foundations which have been making grants to these schools may also be interested in making grants to your school.This process may provide you with additional potential funding sources. For the most current information, the same steps should be followed in researching foundation grants in the bimonthly "Index," published in the philanthropic journal *Foundation News.*

If you were interested in learning about all foundation grants to libraries, the *COMSEARCH Printout* for libraries would provide the fastest and most efficient means of access. Available in paper or microfiche format, *COMSEARCH Printouts* are computer printouts from the Foundation Grants Data Bank in 54 broad subject areas. The printout for libraries lists 394 foundation grants to libraries, information centers, and learning resource centers recorded in 1976. Arranged geographically by foundation location, the printout can be scanned to get a total picture of foundation funding in this subject area or, more specifically, particular types of grants to libraries.

After completing your search through the annual and bimonthly *Grants Index* and/or the *COMSEARCH Printout* for libraries, you could turn to the fields-of-interest index in the back of the *Founda-*

tion Directory. Although limited to foundations that make grants on a national or regional level, this index provides access to these foundations by several broad subject areas, one of which is libraries. Looking under the term "libraries," the researcher is referred to six foundations which indicate in their statements of purpose and activities that they make grants to libraries. The grant seeker might also do well to check those foundations listed under the subject heading "education, higher" and/or "minority groups," to find the names of additional funding sources.

As you research potential funding sources in the *Foundation Directory* and *The Foundation Grants Index,* you should keep in mind the differences in the subject approaches of these two sources. While the former usually indicates the broad fields of interest of a foundation, the latter shows specific grants made by a foundation. This has an important implication for the seeker of library funds. There are several large foundations that make grants to libraries, but for purposes of flexibility in the awarding of grants, they categorize these contributions under the broad headings "education" or "higher education" in their statements of purpose. The entries for these foundations in the fields-of-interest index of the *Directory* will therefore be listed *only* under those headings, and *not* under foundation grants to libraries. The grants of these same foundations, however, will be listed in *The Foundations Grants Index* and can easily be identified by using the key-word index. The point is that the grant seeker would do well to be aware of the capabilities of each research tool in order to use each effectively in conjunction with the other.

Researching Foundations by Geographic Location

For projects with a local scope, the geographic approach is usually the most productive. Suppose that you were looking for funds for support of a small project in your local public library. Your best approach might be to seek out those foundations in your own geographic area, because they would probably be most receptive to the community appeal of your project. The *Foundation Center National Data Book* can be a starting point in a geographic search of foundations. Volume 2 provides a list of more than 21,000 foundations, arranged by state. Next to each foundation's entry is the foundation's total annual grants and the foundation's address. By studying the foundation profiles in a given state, a grant seeker can gain insight into the composition and funding potential of the foundation community in his geographic area. Depending on the number, you might do well to research every foundation in your community, city, or state.

Since most of these foundations are small and have not published information about themselves, your only recourse will be to research them by using IRS information returns 990PF and 990AR. The returns for each foundation you research will include a list of grants for the latest available year. A brief scanning of these lists should indicate which foundations would be the most likely sources of support.

The grant seeker should also be aware of the geographic search capabilities of the *Foundation Directory* and *The Foundation Grants Index* and use them when appropriate. The *Directory's* geographic index provides a list of the large foundations in your city or state. Once specific foundations have been identified, the researcher can quickly scan the purpose and activities section of the entries to ascertain which foundations might be potential donors within the community. *The Foundation Grants Index* can also be searched geographically as the grant records for each foundation are listed by state. It should be remembered, however, that the *Index* contains grant records of $5,000 and over, most of which have been awarded by the larger foundations.

Still another resource to be consulted in a geographic search of foundations is the growing number of state directories of foundations which are currently being published by various organizations. Although these directories vary with respect to content, accuracy, and currency, they provide an additional resource for foundation information. Copies of these directories are available for consultation at the center's New York and Washington, D.C., libraries. Cooperating collections will usually have the directory for their own state, if one exists. Write to the Foundation Center for a bibliography of currently available state directories.

Developing a Proposal

"Strategy" is fine, if you have a proper understanding of what the term means in this context. If it means manipulation in order to achieve an expected response to a formula, it has no place in approaching foundations. Nor does it have a place if it implies the notion that the key factor is "who you know" rather than the merit of your proposal, or "tell them anything, just so you get the money." Cynicism of this kind may work once or twice, but is likely to backfire.

Rather, think of strategy as appropriate formulation and presentation of your ideas in a spirit of openness. Your best strategy lies in a thorough job of home work (that is, researching the basic information about your funding targets), good project leadership, sound and workable ideas, and a strong proposal.

Some matters which may be considered as part of your strategy are (1) the sequence of events in your approach to a foundation and (2) the timing of your proposal submission. After you have learned all you can about a foundation from the public record, you will probably be in a position to determine if a letter or phone call should be your first step in communication. If the foundation puts out an annual report and has a well-defined program statement, you can be fairly confident that it will answer a letter promptly and will give you either encouragement or a clear-cut no. Generally use a letter in these circumstances. The short, written presentation gives you the chance to present your ideas briefly in a concentrated, well-organized form, and this is a definite advantage.

If the foundation does not have a well-defined program state-ment, or if you have reason to believe that the foundation may be interested in your ideas, even though they do not seem to fall into any of their stated categories, a telephone call may be a helpful first step.

The brief letter versus the telephone call may be a matter of temperament or style. If you feel more comfortable with one form than the other, and if you feel that the presentation of your idea can be more effective in one form rather than the other, use it. Each has its pluses and minuses: immediacy versus precision and organization of statement. Generally use the method which is most economical in terms of time and convenience. Of course, do not spend a lot of time developing a lengthy proposal until you are reasonably sure your idea is within the foundation's program scope and the foundation has the financial capability of funding your project. And be sure to note and follow published statements on application procedures which appear in annual reports or other foundation publications.

If you have made your initial inquiry, say, by letter and have not received a reply after a reasonable interval, you may choose between a follow-up by telephone or letter. The purpose is politely to remind the foundation of your communication and that you would like to hear from them. A good way is to add new information or "bring them up to date" on the progress of your program.

Do not be surprised if a foundation does not reply immediately, or even after a long interval. A small staff (or even *no* staff) may be part of the reason. Poor response to mail inquiries has been a common criticism of foundations for many years, but you deserve an answer. It is the least the foundation can do to meet its public responsibility. If you are still determined, a telephone call might be in order, but as you may have discovered, phone numbers for foundations are not always easy to find. They may not be in the telephone directory, and numbers listed in the 990PF may be those of the attorneys who represent the foundation. The telephone numbers of many of the large foundations, however, can now be found in the sixth edition of *Foundation Directory*. Locally, you may have to find someone who knows the officers or trustees of the foundation personally. Library board members or city officials may be of some assistance. All of this will require tact and personal diplomacy, and recognition of the complex human factors involved.

Biographical information in directories or other published sources should be used with great circumspection. Avoid presuming on such knowledge. Trustees may resent offhand mention of irrelevant personal details. Generally, do not address proposals or communications about proposals to trustees unless you have a green light from them or the program officer. Communications of this kind, "out of the blue," often end up in the wastebasket. If a trustee is influenced by your plea, you may win that point but find that the program officer is displeased. Better stick to normal channels and rely as little as possible on personal "ins," unless you are sure of your ground or certain that there is no other way of reaching the decision maker in the foundation.

If your initial contact results in enough interest to warrant further action, you should follow it up with a full proposal as soon as possible. However, determine when the foundation wants it (usually sometime before the next board meeting). A program officer will tell you what the deadlines are, and sometimes this information is published in the annual report. A good proposal will require concentrated days or weeks of preparation; so begin early to avoid a crash effort at the last moment. If you feel you are not ready, you should wait until the next deadline.

If you are making simultaneous applications to several foundations for the same project, the best policy is full disclosure of this fact. It may complicate your negotiations, handling of funds, and reporting later on, but failure to do so may cause embarrassment and loss of credibility.

You know your program and project better than anyone else—at least you should. Therefore we recommend that you do your own information gathering and proposal writing. It will probably produce a better product, and at much less cost, than you could get from outsiders. The proposal that is written by people outside an organization is easily recognizable, foundation officials tell us, and may be in your disfavor, especially if it is evident that you are spending too much money for your outside assistance or if slickness masks your genuine merits. Professional fund-raising counsel of high ethical standards is best utilized in large fund-raising campaigns—for example, those mounted on behalf of an institution such as a college, university, ballet company, or the like. Your own development officer should be involved, of course, but the concept and "case statement" must come from you. Institutional priorities may be a problem if your development department is "saving" foundation X for a much larger or (in their view) much more important project than your library project. Work with your development officer. He or she may make some good suggestions at many points along the way.

The Proposal

There is no universally accepted pattern for proposal planning and writing. Each proposal should be somewhat different from others and will depend on perceptions of the problem, the nature of the project, and what the writer brings to the process in terms of personal resources and points of view. However, there is great similarity in the steps recommended by most writers on the subject. In fact, proposal planning and writing are not markedly different from any kind of problem-solving activity.

In preparing to write a proposal, you must raise a series of questions about (1) your beginning situation, (2) the nature of foundations in general, (3) and specific funding sources.

You might begin by studying two leaflets distributed by the Foundation Center and written by foundation officials with broad experience in the field. Both deal briefly with the two sides of the equation $A + B = C$, in which A is the fund seeker, B the foundation program officer, and C the grant.

Robert A. Mayer considers the preparatory steps in a general way:

1. Study your needs carefully and state your case well, and ask yourself such hard questions as. Is this trip really necessary?
2. Find the right foundation door (the information gathering process we have described).

He then attempts to answer the question "What will the foundation staff member look for in a proposal?" from the differing points of view of large national foundations and local foundations.

Similarly, the Jacquettes present advice to proposal writers under such headings as

1. Clear summary of what is to be accomplished
2. Defense of why this plan is needed
3. Description of the people to be involved
4. Realistic financing scheme
5. Appropriate organizational arrangements.

In the second part of their outline, they sketch the criteria foundations use in assessing proposals.

Read these two leaflets thoughtfully, and discuss their implications with your colleagues. If you decide that foundation funding is a likely possibility for your project, you may need a suggested structure for your proposal if a logical pattern is not already apparent to you.

Two helpful outlines that are often used are readily available in Norton J. Kiritz's "Program Planning and Proposal Writing"[6] and Hillman and Abarbanel's *The Art of Winning Foundation Grants.*[7] Let's look at the eight elements treated by Kiritz, together with some of his comments on each.

Proposal Summary. In writing to a foundation, the summary may be presented as a cover letter or the first paragraph of a letter-type proposal. The summary is probably the first thing a funding source will read. It should be clear, concise, and specific. It should describe who you are, the scope of your project, and the projected cost.

Introduction. This is the section of a proposal where you tell who you are, in which you build your credibility as an organization which should be supported.

Potential funding sources should be selected because of their possible interest in your type of organization or your type of program. Reinforce the connection you see between your interests and those of the funding source.

Problem Statement or Assessment of Need. Now you zero in on the specific problem or problems that you want to solve through the program you are proposing.

Narrow your definition of the problem you want to deal with to something you can hope to accomplish within a reasonable amount of time and with reasonable additional resources.

Document the problem. How do you know that a problem really exists? Don't just assume that "everybody knows this is a problem."

Program Objectives. An objective is a specific, measurable outcome of your program.

Clearly, if you have defined a problem, your objective should offer some relief of the problem.

If you have difficulty defining your objective, try projecting your agency a year or two into the future. What differences would you hope to see between then and now? What changes would have occurred? These changed dimensions may be the objectives of your program.

Methods. Describe the methods you will use—the activities you will conduct to accomplish your objectives.

The informed reviewer wants to know why you have selected these methods. Why do you think they will work?

Evaluation. Evaluation of your program can serve two purposes for your organization. Your program can be evaluated to determine how effective it is in reaching the objectives you have established, in solving the problems you are dealing with. This concept of evaluation is geared toward the results of your program.

Evaluation can also be used as a tool to provide information necessary to make appropriate changes and adjustments in your program as it proceeds.

Measurable objectives set the stage for effective evaluation. If you have difficulty determining what criteria to use in evaluating your program, better take another look at your objectives. They probably aren't very specific.

Budget. Personnel: (1) wages and salaries, (2) fringe benefits, (3) consultants and contract services.

Nonpersonnel: (1) space costs, (2) rental, lease, or purchase of equipment, (3) consumable supplies, (4) travel, (5) telephones, (6) other costs.

Future Funding. Increasingly, funding sources want to know how you will continue your program when their grant runs out.

One good way is to get a local institution or governmental agency to agree to continue to support your program, should it demonstrate the desired results. A plan to generate funds through the project itself (such as fees for services that will build up over a year or two, subscriptions to publications, etc.) is an excellent plan.

Each of these sections requires careful thinking and writing. The entire proposal should probably go through several drafts and a critical review by others in your organization or "outsiders" whose judgment you can rely on.

Creativity

After reading the manuals and listening to the authorities and their informed opinions, you return to yourself and your own encounter with your environment. At this point you have a choice, one you always face: of doing it "by the book" or of investing yourself in the task.

Your best work is likely to arise from reliance on an initial, spontaneous expression of simple common sense which aims at a creative adjustment of a social or organizational issue.

Conventional solutions to problems depend on seeing the issues from a so-called realistic point of view, an accepted framework based on old policies and vested interests, which usually results in a choice between the "lesser of two evils." The "creative" approach to a difficulty is just the opposite: it tries to advance the problem to a different level by discovering or inventing a new, third approach that is essential to the issue and spontaneously recommends itself. This takes courage, because society resists such innovative approaches. Those who advance them are often called escapist, impractical, utopian, or unrealistic.

But what is creativity? Does it apply to mundane things, like writing a foundation proposal? And can it be learned?

There are many definitions of creativity and all of them seem to agree that it is the process by which original patterns are formed and expressed. It may occur anywhere in human affairs, and not just in notable achievements in the arts and sciences. Abraham Maslow says, "A first rate soup is more creative than a second rate painting," and "From one man, I learned that constructing a business organization could be a creative activity. From a young athlete, I learned that a perfect tackle could be as aesthetic a product as a sonnet and could be approached in the same creative spirit."

As you work on your funding proposal, ask yourself if your approach is predictable and repetitive, or if it is based on a new perception of the problem.

Your proposal may give you the opportunity for a new arrangement of familiar elements in your working environment. Don't settle for accepted ways of thinking about the obvious. Experiment with apparent disorder—that is, with the unknown. Then return to your finite problem-solving environment. Some of the new combinations you have envisioned may be workable and can be translated into new structures of social value. The imaginative process of formulating your plan will enhance the value of the product both for you and those you are trying to help.

Another way of seeing the difference between solutions which merely work and creative solutions to problems is to consider the difference between commercial entertainment and art. Art explains; entertainment exploits. Art is freedom from the conditions of memory. Entertainment depends on a present conditioned by the past; it gives us what we want. Art gives us what we don't know we want. To confront a work of art is to confront one's self—but aspects of one's self previously unrecognized.[9]

It is exactly that quality of art which you and the foundation program officer should be seeking in a proposal. Neither should be crowd pleasers—mere entertainers—but artists who are working for new perspectives that release more creative energy.

The greatest challenge of fund raising is not just getting a pot full of dollars for something tried and true, which leaves things exactly as they were, but finding the means to bring about notable changes in people and social structures—something of value which we didn't even know we wanted before we set our minds to the problem.

Notes

1. Marianna O. Lewis, ed., *The Foundation Directory* (6th ed.; New York: The Foundation Center, 1977).

2. F. Emerson Andrews, *Philanthropic Foundations* (New York: Russell Sage Foundation, 1956).

3. Lewis, *The Foundation Directory.*

4. American Association of Fund-Raising Counsel, *Giving, USA: 1975 Annual Report* (New York: AAFRC, 1975).

5. Judith B. Margolin, *About Foundations* (rev. ed.; New York: The Foundation Center, 1977).

6. Reprinted from *Grantsmanship Center News* (Jan. 1974).

7. Howard Hillman and Karin Abarbanel, *The Art of Winning Foundation Grants* (New York: Vanguard Press, 1975).

8. Quoted in Don Fabun, *You and Creativity* (Beverly Hills, Calif.: Glencoe Press, 1969), pp. 4–5.

9. Gene Youngblood, *Expanded Cinema* (New York: Dutton, 1970), pp. 59–65.

Chapter 12

Operating within a Parent Institution

**Patricia Senn Breivik
and E. Burr Gibson**

Libraries that serve the needs of a particular institution, such as a college, university or school, frequently have a number of opportunities to assist in fund-raising endeavors. Often the parent institution has a full-time development officer and staff whose specialized training and experience can be made available to the library. Often there is an established and well-maintained list of donors to the parent institution, and, finally, the library can often benefit from the established and positive reputation of the parent institution.

At multifaceted institutions, it is usually easier to gain visibility and therefore access to volunteer leaders, by utilizing the aura of association with the parent institution. This will require involving the principal officers and the trustees in the program and at appropriate functions. Don't miss the opportunity to do so. In this way the library will be able to gain access to affluent individuals.

Such advantages are not without potential problems, however. First of all, it is essential to develop and maintain an ongoing positive relationship with the development officer. This will include keeping him/her informed of fund-raising activities which are being contemplated and running the risk of being informed that a particular foundation or donor is being "saved" for another project.

Another problem is that few development offices are adequately staffed, which means that if a library is going to benefit from its expertise, it will require the library's being placed high on the institution's list of priorities. This may take considerable time and effort, in and of itself, before a library can even begin fund raising.

Besides fund-raising activities specifically directed at the library, it is also important to arouse (and keep aroused) the development officer's sensitivity to the fact that most grant proposals and fund-raising objectives should have a materials/equipment component built in for the library. How many new programs have been established in colleges and schools without adequate provision for support materials?

There is also a danger that serious competition for fund-raising support may develop. Every fund-raising program that functions within a large institution should have clear guidelines as to how the program will be handled in relation to other programs under way and/or planned by the parent institution. Failing to establish agreed-to guidelines can lead to chaos and failure. A cooperative, rather than a competitive, approach to fund raising among departments or units of an institution should be sought by all concerned. The library, however, is uniquely suited to fare well under cooperative efforts since its services and resources can be clearly shown in support of almost any aspect or program of the parent institution.

The cultivation of the development officer has both a formal and an informal aspect. On the formal side, library priorities will have to be determined, and it will have to be made clear how they relate to the larger objectives and goals of the parent institution. Clearly, they must appear to be a part of a well-conceived plan. This is particularly true when large gifts are sought, as donors will be rightly concerned about ongoing institutional support for programs they fund. Nor will programs appear to be important to donors if they are not clearly important to the major officers of the institution. Since their jobs depend to a certain extent upon a good track record, development officers will also want to support projects which have both strong institutional support and a good chance of being successful.

The informal approach includes inviting the development officer out for lunch or dinner and building a personal relationship with him/her in other nonofficial contacts as well. Obviously, he/she should be regularly issued invitations to any special library events and always made to feel like an honored guest. Such contacts should facilitate support for the library's fund-raising activities, and may even provide informal suggestions as to likely contacts from time to time.

Time should also be spent with the administrators of new and expanding programs or any other individuals likely to be involved in seeking outside funds. Suggestions at the right moment as to how additional resources could enrich their programs, plus an offer to supply the price tag for their use, can result in a library component's being built into proposals beyond the direct control of the library.

A few large university libraries employ full-time fund raisers on their staffs. These people are given the responsibilities which usually fall to the director for spearheading fund-raising activities and for coordinating the library's efforts with the development officer. One such case is the library at Northwestern University, which, during the first three years of having a full-time development officer on its staff, raised over $3 million, primarily in program money. Ted Welch, the development officer, said that the success of the fund-raising program had in turn strengthened the library's political clout on campus, because the library, which had always been perceived as a consumer of university resources, was now seen as a producer of funds.

Welch's efforts also include an ongoing effort to build enthusiasm among the staff for fund-raising activities. Recently, all librarians were asked what they would wish for if more money were available to the library. Their responses were placed in a "Wish Book" and are consulted as potential donors are contacted and/or gifts come in.

As already implied, insofar as possible the tone set by the library in relation to other units should be cooperation in fund-raising, not competition. This attitude is particularly crucial in small situations where personal interactions are more frequent. In the school situation, however, where the Parent-Teacher Association might be working on band uniforms and the basketball coach working on something to support the team's trips, it won't be possible to avoid all semblances of competition. But unless the librarian believes that the library's contribution to the objectives of the school are of far less importance than band uniforms and trips by the basketball team, the library's needs must be presented—for those who do most of the selling and those who tell their stories most often are the ones who get the money.

In such a situation, it is important to emphasize that the fund-seeking programs are very different in nature and therefore will appeal to different interests. Moreover, competition cannot be assumed, since it has been proved that people will give over and over again if they feel that their money will be used wisely.

Friends groups are quite possible within a large institutional setting. Here again, the library will want to work within the existing framework, whether it be with an alumni officer, alumni association, PTA, or other group. Sometimes it will make more sense to establish a completely separate group; sometimes a subgroup of an already established organization will better serve the library's interests. Checking what other nearby libraries do, which operate under similar circumstances, can provide helpful suggestions. (An example of the potential fund-raising success of such groups is given in the case study from Oakland University in chapter 14.)

All of the pre-fund-raising activities discussed in this chapter demand heavy outlays of time on the part of the director. This is one reason why the commitment to fund raising must be fairly widespread in the library; otherwise, the director's "socializing" at the expense of other duties may cause morale problems. Fund raising takes time and money. Some of both may be absorbed by the development office, but only after the initial commitment and follow-through by the library.

Particular care must also be taken during the pre-fund-raising stage to reach agreement as to how the monies raised will affect the present level of library funding. An understanding needs to be reached with the central administration, and *put into writing,* that the amounts will not be deducted from the funds appropriated for the library's operations. This agreement should be reached before pre-fund-raising activities are begun.

To a large extent, the ease with which a library that serves a particular institution enters into fund raising will depend upon the esteem in which it and/or its director is held within the parent institution. The library which is already perceived as a dynamic, integral part of the larger body will find it easier to open the necessary doors. Libraries that offer services which directly support its institution and are somewhat beyond the traditional library role will find it easier to make an interesting, compelling case statement.

Fund raising by libraries will also be facilitated if its parent institution has clearly stated goals and objectives to which it may relate. Lacking such, the library will have to build its case in more general educational terms, for example, the role of the library in preparing people for lifelong learning. Usually there are written documents such as college catalogs which contain general educational objectives which can be quoted for this purpose.

Of course, the quality of the development office will vary from institution to institution. Some will simply have more expertise than others. For this reason, every library should be concerned when a new development officer is recruited. Active involvement in the recruitment procedure can lay a good foundation for future involvements.

As the library begins to have successes, they should be communicated internally as well as externally. Those who have been directly involved should be appropriately thanked. When the program goals are achieved, be sure to share the bows with all who helped in any way. This will not be the library's last fund-raising effort, and when it decides to launch the next campaign, most of these people will be willing to help again because they were meaningfully involved, kept informed along the way, and properly thanked for their efforts.

Chapter 13

Fund Raising for
University Libraries

Andrew J. Eaton

This paper grows out of several convictions about the subject. First, that fund raising has been a relatively neglected aspect of university librarianship. Very little has been written about it, and most librarians have, for various reasons, considered it none of their business. Second, that this situation is gradually changing, primarily because of financial pressures on university libraries. Some librarians have already become more involved in seeking outside funds, and many others will be doing this in the future. Third, that there are potontialitios for library fund raising which will amply repay those librarians who are willing to devote their time and effort to it. Fourth, that librarians who want to become involved need certain basic information about sources of funds and approaches to prospective donors which they can readily obtain from colleagues and from development office staff members who have been working in the field.

These notions, held for some time in tentative form, have been strengthened during the past year in which the writer, under a grant from the Council on Library Resources, attempted to learn about the subject by reading and by talking with librarians, development officers, and people in foundations and government. The conclusions presented here are not the results of a systematic research study.

This article is reprinted with permission of the publisher from the September 1971 issue of *College & Research Libraries*, pp. 351–61.

Rather, they are the pieced-together impressions and the distilled experience of many people who have pondered, written, and practiced in the field of academic library fund raising.

First, a word about the financial problems of university librarians. There is abundant evidence that, like the universities they serve, academic libraries are under severe and growing financial pressures. This applies to all kinds of institutions: public and private, strong and weak, old and emerging. Costs of operation are rising steadily. According to statistics published by the Association of Research Libraries, thirty-two university libraries spent over $3 million each in 1969–70, and twenty-three others spent between $2 million and $3 million. The reasons for this are familiar—the demand for more materials and services by users, the rising costs of books and staff, the increase in the number of books published, the opening of new fields of scholarly interest, the need for specialists on library staffs, the pressure to automate, etc. Expensive as libraries are now, they are expected to cost even more in the future. Harvard, which spent $7.6 million in 1968–69, predicts that the library budget in 1976 will be at least $14.6 million. Yale estimates that its library operating budget of $4.5 million in 1968 would have to double every five years if all the requested books and services were to be made available.

Faced with increases of this kind in many areas of their operations, universities across the country are finding that growth in income is simply not keeping pace with rising costs. The inevitable result is retrenchment, and libraries are beginning to feel the effects. In many institutions the rate of annual budget increase has dropped from 15 or 20 percent, common several years ago, to 3 or 4 percent, which is even too little to offset price increases. Some libraries are facing actual budget cuts in personnel or books, or even in both categories. The prospect is that the financial situation will worsen before it improves.

What is the university librarian to do under these circumstances? He should certainly not be expected to apologize for the fact that libraries cost money; he is no more responsible for this than the graduate dean is responsible for increases in the research budget. He should continue to look for ways to reduce costs through such means as relying on other collections for highly specialized materials, using cataloging information developed by the Library of Congress under the National Program for Acquisitions and Cataloging, and experimenting with other cooperative ventures. He should hope that his institution will scrutinize its academic program to bring it in line with anticipated resources. Also, he should consider the possibility of raising some money from outside sources for library support.

Although most university libraries receive the bulk of their support from appropriated funds, gifts from outside sources have long been an important item of income, particularly in private institutions. In a survey made in 1956–57 Powell found that twenty-two university libraries received $1,175,631 in cash gifts that year and $906,842 in endowment income from earlier gifts.[1] This constituted 18.5 percent of the total expenditures of the private university libraries in the sample and 2.5 percent of the expenditures of the state-supported libraries. In the absence of any newer studies it is impossible to say how the picture has changed in the years since 1956. Since Powell's sample of ten private universities included seven ivy-league institutions, the 18.5 percent is undoubtedly too high to accept as a national average for private university libraries.

It is probably fair to say that the typical university librarian's attitude toward fund raising is that this is a responsibility which belongs primarily to others—the development office, the president and the board of trustees. The librarian has been willing and, in many cases, eager to work at the job of acquiring gifts of books, and he has devoted his time to friends of the library organizations in the hope of obtaining both collections and annual income from dues. But in seeking cash gifts he has hesitated to take the initiative, preferring to leave this job to others. When the development office suggests the names of prospective donors, the librarian responds by proposing appropriate projects. He may know a few donors who are keenly interested in the library and whose devotion is such that he feels free to approach them when special needs arise. But toward other prospects his role has been a passive one, influenced perhaps by the view that a librarian who devotes his time aggressively to raising money is straying outside his field. In some universities the development office has apparently encouraged this view, hoping to keep all fund-raising activities under tight central control.

This is not to say that some university librarians have not been active and successful in raising money. In at least one institution (Harvard) it has long been understood that an important part of the librarian's responsibility is building financial support, even to the extent of raising several million dollars for a major plant addition. In a few of the other private universities, librarians have devoted considerable time to donor cultivation and fund raising. Some of the younger directors who have recently taken over major private ARL libraries are alert to the possibilities and eager to exploit them.[2]

The librarian who is willing to assume the role of entrepreneur in seeking funds has several factors in his favor. His willingness to help meet the university's financial problems will be appreciated by the administration. He will have plenty of company within most private universities where deans are being increasingly pressured to raise money for their own operations. He will be entering a field where success is by no means assured, but where the potential is demonstrably great; there are many individuals, foundations, and other sources of funds capable of responding to imaginative proposals carefully tailored to their individual requirements. Library needs are so diverse that they can be packaged in numerous ways. The task of matching donors and needs is one which can challenge the talents of the most imaginative and creative librarian. It is the librarian who is often in the best position to speak convincingly of library needs and of the opportunities they offer to discriminating donors.

Some librarians may hesitate to become fund raisers on the ground that they are not suited for the job by personality or temperament. If they had been cut out to be salesmen, they may argue, they would not have chosen librarianship as a career. But while fund raising does involve selling, persuading prospective donors to give money for libraries does not necessarily require a brash, hucksterish approach. More important are qualities which many academic librarians have in abundance—sensitivity, patience, imagination, tact, integrity, and enthusiasm for one's product. Willingness to take something of an entrepreneurial view of the librarian's job is also essential, but this too is not uncommon in the profession.

The librarian entering the fund-raising field must realize that he will not be doing the job alone. In any university there will be many other people working with him—development office staff, other staff members in the library, volunteers, friends (organized or not), and, of course, the president and members of the board of trustees. The success of the institution's fund-raising efforts will depend not only upon the ability of the various people involved but also on their willingness to work together, on their understanding of each other's roles, and on the degree to which their efforts can be coordinated in pursuit of a common goal.

As the group primarily responsible for institutional fund raising, the development office normally consists of several professionals each responsible for a particular area (e.g., foundations, alumni, corporations, bequests, etc.). In addition to these assignments by source of funds, some staff members may have responsibility for working with major divisions of the university such as the library. Development officers in many institutions apparently want the heads of various academic divisions to play an active part in fund raising. They see their own role, in fact, as one of assisting and coordinating rather than doing the whole job themselves. They are prepared to screen donors and assess their potential, help recruit and train volunteers, secure clearance on prospects, and assist in drafting proposals. But they look to deans and other administrative officers and faculty to take the initiative in suggesting proposals, in identifying prospects, and in making presentations.

Relationships between the library (and other academic divisions) and the development office are apparently in need of improvement in many universities. The librarian should make an effort to understand how the development office works, to know the staff, and to see that they are fully informed about library needs. He will get help from the development staff if he demonstrates a willingness to devote his time to fund raising, if he abides by the institution's policies governing approaches to prospective donors, and if he has a clear understanding of the division of labor between the library and the development office in making appeals for funds.

With growing pressures on university budgets, development office personnel will undoubtedly be concentrating more and more on seeking unrestricted funds. If so, they will have less time to raise money for particular divisions of the university. This should mean that any of them who have been reluctant in the past to involve others in the fund-raising process will now welcome those deans and librarians who are willing to try to raise money for their own areas.

In addition to depending on the development office, the librarian will do well to draw upon personnel within his own staff. In large libraries a number of staff members may have the aptitude for and an interest in fund raising. The head of rare books or special collections is often a person who is sensitive both to needs and to fund-raising possibilities.The acquisitions librarian is in a good position to participate in developing proposals based on needs for collection development.Other staff members with a flair for public relations or with extensive contacts in the community may be able to help. A staff committee on fund raising is a way in which the talents of all interested staff members can be brought to bear on the problem.

A library wanting to make a major effort to raise money should consider having its own development officer. A well-qualified person could pay his way many times over. He could be either a professional in the field or a librarian. A professional would have to depend on the library staff for developing proposals, but he would keep in touch with both sources of funds and prospective donors and he would have a part in presentations. Short of creating a full-time position, a library might employ a half-time person who could work in the area of development. Such a person could investigate promising sources of funds and help prepare proposals. Either a full-time or a half-time person would profit by having the help of a capable assistant who could do the detailed work involved in maintaining prospect files and in assembling information needed for presentations. In fact, this type of help seems essential under any staffing arrangement where a librarian is trying to raise money. A person with public relations or volunteer fund-raising experience would be well qualified for assisting in a library fund-raising program.

In addition to the development office and the librarian and his staff, other people within the university should be concerned with raising money for library purposes. The president is normally the university's chief fund raiser, and his support of the library's efforts is essential. Few presidents have the enthusiasm for library support displayed by Franklin Murphy (Kansas and UCLA), Herman Wells (Indiana), or Harry Ransom (Texas), but many of them have a firm commitment to library development on which the librarian can count in his efforts to seek donors and make presentations. Members of the board of trustees who have a special interest in the library can also be helpful. All board members are normally called upon by the development office to pave the way for presentations by calling foundation or corporation executives or individuals whom they know personally. Finally, the faculty can be most helpful both in drafting proposals and in identifying prospects. Some faculty members will have a flair for thinking of gift opportunities, identifying prospective donors, and making a case for library support.

Volunteers from the community are an essential part of any fund-raising program, and the librarian should see to it that they are enlisted and put to work. Their usefulness lies not only in their ability to make gifts themselves but also in their knowledge of prospects and their willingness to speak up for the library's needs and to ask others to help meet them. Volunteers may be used in various ways. An informal advisory or consulting relationship may be set up with one or more alumni or friends who have a special interest in the library, a flair for money raising, and the time provided by full or semi-retirement to devote to a library fund-raising program. Such an arrangement can be highly beneficial in educating librarians about the realities of raising money and the ways of adapting techniques of salesmanship to the academic world.

Organizing volunteers into committees or friends groups is an approach which the librarian fund raiser should consider carefully. The visiting committee is a device long used at Harvard which is now being tried at other universities (Carnegie-Mellon, California Institute of Technology, Duke, etc.). Harvard has a visiting committee for each department including the university library. They range in size from five to thirty or more members, many of whom are neither alumni nor connected with the university in any other way. They tend to be people with money, influence, and/or prominence in a particular field. The visiting committee is viewed as a way of informing a group of people about the work of a department, of getting their ideas and criticisms, and of enlisting their help in increasing the department's effectiveness.[3]

Harvard's Visiting Committee on the University Library consists of thirty-two members, including business executives and bankers, book collectors, a publisher, an author, a foundation executive, several attorneys, and the distinguished librarian of another ivy-league university. Most of them were appointed, presumably, on recommendation of the librarian. The committee normally meets once a year on a weekend in the spring. Wives are invited, and social activity is pleasantly combined with business. The staff informs the committee about progress, problems, and financial needs. The committee is expected to submit an informal report annually and a formal written report every three years. The chairman of the committee is a member of the Board of Overseers, and reports are made to the Board. A visiting committee consisting primarily of librarians can be useful to the library staff but it is not likely to carry much weight with the university administration or to win support from outside sources. Some development officers feel that visiting committees should be used not primarily for fund raising but more as a way of involving influential people in university activities. The latter, of course, is an important aspect of long-range donor cultivation.

More common than visiting committees by far is the Friends of the Library organization. Many university libraries have them, and some of them are quite successful with membership reaching 500 or 600. The annual dues income is a useful source of funds with which to supplement the book budget. Income may amount to as much as $25,000 a year in a few libraries, but more commonly it will not exceed $5,000. Less tangible but possibly more important in the long run is the opportunity provided by the organization to acquaint bookish and/or wealthy friends with the library's role and needs. A successful friends group requires a considerable investment of time on the part of the library staff. There should be some individual, either on the library staff or among the friends, who has the enthusiasm, the time, and the skill to keep the organization alive and aware of its objectives. Even with an abundance of staff care and volunteer talent there is a danger that the organization will become merely another outlet for the interest of dilettante alumni. One experienced librarian says that the first ten to twelve years are always difficult for friends groups. The decision to start a new organization should be made with full recognition of the attendant problems.

The sources from which libraries may obtain funds include foundations, private individuals (alumni and friends), corporations and business firms, and government agencies. Foundations have traditionally given money for library purposes, and they are still a potential source well worth attention.[4] It is estimated that there are 24,000 foundations in the United States. This number includes a relatively small group of large, professionally managed foundations such as Ford, Rockefeller, Mellon, and a much larger group of family foundations. Some of the major foundations (e.g., Kresge) have made recent gifts to libraries, but most of them have turned their attention in other directions. The family foundations now appear to constitute a more promising source of funds. The Tax Reform Act of 1969 requires that by 1975 all foundations must pay out annually an amount equal to 6 percent of the market value of their assets. Since fewer than half of the foundations have been meeting this standard, foundation giving should increase over the next few years. The act also requires that foundations prepare annual reports and make them available to the public. This should greatly simplify the job of obtaining current information about small foundations.

In approaching foundations the librarian should prepare a list of prospects, identify the people who make the decisions about grants, and decide on the best approach to them. In assembling information about foundations it is often worthwhile to consult tax returns. Copies of the 990-A forms filled out by foundations are on file in the Foundation Center in New York and in its regional depositories across the country. Many small foundations seem to make their grants in November and December at the end of the tax year, often on the basis of requests on hand at the time.

Manning Pattillo, president of the Foundation Center, believes that American foundations are going through a period of change.[5] He forecasts a slowdown in the number of new foundations created, an increase in the number of foundations administered by professional staff, sharpening of foundation purposes with more emphasis on problem-solving and less on general support of organizations, keener competition among applicants for foundation support, more attention to environmental problems, more supervision of grantees, and more evaluation of the results of grants. These changes appear to have no special implications for libraries, but they suggest that obtaining grants may be somewhat more difficult than it has been in the past.

Private individuals who give to university libraries are often alumni of the institution, but they may be businessmen or wealthy

residents of the community who are inspired by an imaginative proposal to create a memorial or simply to make possible some socially
useful project involving books or library facilities. There are many
prospective donors to whom libraries can have a strong appeal. The
problem is to identify them and to cultivate their interest. Suggestions of names may be sought from development office staff, from
members of friends groups, from library staff members, from faculty,
from alumni office personnel, etc. Lists of members of local cultural
organizations (the historical society, symphony, and the art museum)
may offer suggestions. With a prospect list in hand the librarian must
search for additional information about each person. Directories,
local history books, and the development office files are possible
sources, but these must frequently be supplemented by personal
inquiries directed to friends and volunteer fund raisers who are
widely acquainted in the community.

Corporate giving is channeled primarily through corporate
foundations. There are now about 2,000 such foundations in the
United States, and nearly three-fourths of all corporate contributions
flowed through them in 1969. Many of these foundations will be
preempted by the university development office for solicitation of
unrestricted gifts. Some business firms with subject interests may be
prospects for library gift proposals in the areas with which they are
concerned (e.g., a printing firm may respond to a request to help
develop a collection in the history of printing). The program recently
set up by the Sears, Roebuck Foundation to assist private colleges and
universities in strengthening their book collections is an example of
enlightened corporate philanthropy which will benefit many institutions.

During the 1960s the federal government made an encouraging
beginning in the support of academic libraries through grants for
both materials and facilities. Funds appropriated fell far short of the
amounts needed, but many institutions were helped. These funds
have recently been reduced and there is no reason to believe that
increased appropriations will be provided in the next few years. The
whole federal approach to aiding higher education, moreover, is being
reconsidered, and there is a possibility that future funding may take
the form of block grants to institutions rather than grants for specific
purposes such as libraries. This would mean that libraries would
have to compete with other parts of the university for available funds.

While federal aid to libraries generally is being cut back, assistance to needy and disadvantaged libraries may be increased in the
immediate future. The Association of College and Research Libraries
Grants Program has been trying to help such institutions in recent

years by awarding small grants from money collected primarily from the U.S. Steel Foundation. It is interesting that a panel of fund-raising consultants has recently recommended that institutional grants be discontinued under this program and that the available funds be used instead to teach librarians how to do their own fund raising, chiefly by tapping federal and state government sources.[6]

Having made arrangements for coworkers and familiarized him-self with sources of funds the librarian should consider what ap-proaches he will use to raise money. One useful first step is to prepare a five-year plan. This plan should outline objectives, identify long- and short-range goals, specify priorities, and include a timetable. To permit building up momentum, several easily obtainable goals should be set for the first six months or a year. This plan should be discussed with the development office, and ways of achieving the objectives should be agreed upon. Among the approaches which de-serve consideration are large and small proposals aimed at specific individuals or foundations, a memorial fund or tribute fund for rela-tively small contributions by a large number of donors, bequests, and provisions for library support attached to faculty grant proposals.

In preparing gift proposals the librarian should identify particu-lar library needs which can be packaged to appeal to donor interests. New fields of collection development such as Slavic, Asian, Latin American or African studies, Urban and Regional History, or Judaica offer attractive possibilities. A year's fund-raising activity might include a number of proposals of this nature, each with a price tag of $75,000 to $150,000. Or, a donor may be asked to underwrite the on-going development of a collection in a traditional field such as art history, musicology, or engineering. Here the appropriateness of an endowment to yield $5,000 to $10,000 a year can be stressed. Memo-rial opportunities can be attached to each proposal if this seems desirable.

All proposals, of course, need not be of such magnitude. Many smaller packages can be prepared, consisting of a major reference work, the back file of a journal, or a reprint collection on a particular subject. These may cost anywhere from a few hundred to a few thousand dollars. The library should have a sizable number of such proposals which can be presented to donors with special subject interests.

In presenting the larger proposals care must be taken to describe the gift opportunity in a clear and convincing fashion. It is usually desirable to do this in a one-page statement which describes the collection or facility wanted, the use to be made of it, its relation to the university's overall objectives, the amount of money involved, and the relevance of the project to the interests of the prospective donor. It is important, if possible, to show how the gift can make a crucial difference in the quality of a particular program, making it distinctive or outstanding in comparision with others in the same field.

Proposals should be presented only after prospective donors have been thoroughly researched and cleared with the development office. Information needed about them includes their personal and family backgrounds, friends and business connections, hobbies and other interests, previous gifts, if any, giving potential and attitude toward the university. Ideally, donors should be approached with projects which will have an emotional appeal for them. The actual presentation should be made only after the way has been prepared by a person who has some influence with the prospect. If the librarian makes the presentation, this person might well be asked to accompany him.

The presentation of the proposal should emphasize the opportunity for the donor rather than the library's desperate needs. Discussion of budget cuts and financial stringency usually has no place in a conversation about a possible gift. It is sometimes desirable to pre sent the project as an idea and invite the prospective donor's reaction. The donor should be asked for an amount large enough to challenge him. If it is too much, he will say so. This is better than asking for too little. Once the donor has accepted the proposal, a written version of the agreement should be prepared for his signature. When the project has been completed the librarian should give the donor a report on it. Fund raisers emphasize that prospects who decline the first opportunity should be asked again, perhaps with some variation in the proposal. They agree that a person who gives once is a prime candidate for resolicitation, since he has already committed himself to the library's cause.

Another approach is the memorial fund or tribute fund through which alumni and friends of the university can give money in honor or in memory of others. The approach is based on the idea that the gift of a book to the university library can be used as a way of paying tribute to another person. The plan involves considerable correspondence which is often handled by a central gift record office. Appropriate cards can be designed to acknowledge gifts and to inform those who are being honored. Special bookplates are usually inserted in volumes purchased with gift funds. A properly publicized project of this kind can bring in between $5,000 and $10,000 a year when it becomes established.

Deferred giving is an approach to fund raising which is receiving increasing attention from development officers, and the librarian should find a way of using it. The development office staff member responsible for bequests should be fully informed about the library's needs and should be given descriptions of the kind of projects which could be presented to donors who are preparing wills. An effort should be made either by the development office or by the library to inform lawyers and trust officers, especially those who are alumni, about the opportunities in the library for those making bequests. Fund-raising brochures produced by the library should mention bequest opportunities and perhaps suggest appropriate language.

Another approach to obtaining funds is to ask for library support as a part of faculty grant proposals. The problem here is finding out about proposals early enough to persuade the faculty to consider library implications. The central office responsible for processing grant requests may be able to alert the library to proposals in preparation. If a particular project involves a need for library support, the costs of this support should be included in the proposal. One university adds 15 percent for library costs to every grant proposal submitted to a foundation. Occasionally it may be appropriate to include funds for the acquisition of books as a major component of a project to improve teaching and research in a particular area. This has been done by some universities in their proposals for expansion of area study programs.

The recognition of donors is an important aspect of fund raising to which the librarian must give attention. A few donors want to remain anonymous, taking satisfaction in the knowledge that they have contributed to some worthwhile endeavor. Most of them, however, want to be recognized in some way, and the form of recognition may determine whether or not the donor will respond favorably to the proposal. In making a decision the librarian will take account of various factors: the importance of the gift, the donor's wishes, the cost involved, and the desirability of setting precedents which may have to be followed with other donors in the future.

The use of a special bookplate is one of the easiest and most common ways of recognizing the donor of funds for books. Attractive plates can be designed, and the donor's ideas can often be incorporated in them. Exhibits of gift books are appreciated by donors, especially where the exhibit opening is accompanied by a reception to which they can invite friends. Plaques are used frequently to record donors' names in the library, and a large gift may justify naming a part of the building for the donor or someone designated by him, with a portrait or bust attached. A donor's name may also be perpetuated by naming in his honor a collection, an annual award, a lectureship, a book collection contest, or a series of publications. Some universities present citations to major donors or honor them by having dinners to which trustees, administration, and faculty are invited.

Publications may be used effectively to announce gifts and to give recognition to donors. Most libraries use university publications (newspapers, alumni magazines, etc.) to publicize gifts and to call attention to the idea of giving for library purposes. A substantial gift will usually justify a special brochure or exhibit catalog, or an article in the Friends of the Library publication. Where a library does not issue a regular journal for Friends, it may consider publishing an occasional newsletter describing new gift collections and additions to older ones. This is a way in which donors' names can be mentioned, both for their gratification and as a stimulus to other donors.

Along with efforts devoted directly to fund raising should go a continuous program of library publicity and long-term cultivation of donors. Local news media and general university publications as well as the library's own publications should be used to the fullest extent possible to call attention to the library's role, needs, accomplishments, and aspirations. A member of the library staff should be given responsibility for initiating and coordinating all library publicity. Cultivation of donors and prospective donors requires finding ways of keeping in touch and encouraging participation in university and library activities. Friends or prospective donors should receive invitations to university and library functions and should be made in every way possible to feel that they are a part of the university community. This is time consuming and often apparently unproductive, but it is a necessary part of a library fund-raising program.

Notes

1. B. E. Powell, "Sources of Support for Libraries in American Universities," in *The Library in the University* (University of Tennessee Library Lectures, 1949–1966) (Hamden, Conn.: Shoe String Press, 1967), pp. 173–94.
2. David Kaser, "The Golden Touch, or the Gentle Art of Raising Money," *Stechert-Hafner Book News* 19 (May 1965): 109-10.
3. Harvard College, Board of Overseers, *Committee Assignments, 1969–70.*
4. Lawrence Heilprin and Corinne Lynch, "Foundation Support of Library Activity," *Bowker Annual of Library and Book Trade Information, 1969* (New York: Bowker, 1969), pp. 138–42.
5. Manning Pattillo, "Foundations in the 70s Will Undergo Many Changes," *Fund Raising Management* 2 (July-August 1970): 11–13.
6. Advisory Panel on the Grants Program of the ACRL, *Final Report* (Oct. 1, 1969), mimeo.

Chapter 14

Three Case Studies

The number of case studies in this book which have been successful in fund raising could have been considerably expanded. The editors solicited the following three, as each epitomizes basic fundraising concepts which they thought worth emphasizing.

The case study of the Portland (Maine) Public Library is a prime example of the multifaceted approach that can and should be taken by many libraries in seeking to expand their funding base. The library has increased its tax base, gotten grants, completed a capital fund campaign, and worked with a friends group. At the time of this writing, it was planning the establishment of an annual fund campaign.

The Oakland University Library case study not only emphasizes the principle of increasing returns from fund-raising efforts by building upon previous years' efforts but underscores the potential of volunteer friends groups in serious fund-raising endeavors. Since friends groups most often are thought of in terms of public libraries, the editors were particularly pleased that a university friends group developed an activity which for several years has opened the social season in Detroit.

The final case study (Lincoln Center) is of a specialized research library which has capitalized on its uniqueness and its location. The amount of detail underscores the importance of planning for effective fund raising.

The editors' research failed to uncover any major or unique examples of fund raising for school libraries. The Knapp Foundation grant, which poured $1,130,000 into a selected group of school libraries in the 1960s, was secured through the efforts of the American Association of School Librarians. Of course, over the years many schools have benefited from federal LSCA (Library Services and Construction Act) funds and/or the efforts of parent/teacher organizations. It would appear, however, that staffing patterns of most school libraries are a severe deterrence to their seeking alternative funding sources to support their programs.

Fund Raising at the Portland Public Library

Edward V. Chenevert

At Portland, Maine, the public library has tripled its budget, doubled its staff, built two new branch libraries, added extensive outreach services, a big bookmobile with an elevator for wheelchairs, handicapped services, learners' advisory services, and now we are building a new $6 million central library. All of this in a community of 65,000 people, sorely beset by the pressures of the local property tax—a community with $40 million of capital needs every year but managing to fund only about $1.7 million of these needs.

What can be learned from the Portland experience? How can one plunge into the troubled waters of library finance without drowning? What is the magic behind the green door of library funding?

I learned a phrase from a wise counselor of problem teen-agers, who said, "You work with what you've got." He meant, of course, that you start where you are and build on what is already there.

When I became Portland's library director in 1970, I took a look at the budget. I learned that the library was a nonprofit agency chartered by the state of Maine in 1867. Support derived from a mixture of sources, including the city of Portland. The city's share is listed as a "contribution to an outside agency." By 1970, this contribution had risen to 80 percent of the total budget. True, there were endowments of over a million dollars, but most of this was restricted to the purchase of books. Miscellaneous income, such as fines, gifts, etc., accounted for the balance of the library's income. I was shocked to discover that the state of Maine's contribution was only $200 yearly, and for which several pages of statistics had to be submitted.

A dismal picture began to emerge, including the level of staff salaries—$6,000 for a beginning professional! Having recently come into the library from the business world, I began to look upon librarians as "downtrodden masses" and the library as "the neglected relative" of the city establishment. As one city counselor later put it, "Until Eddie came along, the library used to come to city hall every year with a shoe box, looking for a handout."

If 80 percent of the library's budget derived from the city, my first order of business was to "build my blocks" with the city officials. I had lunch with the city manager and waxed so effusive about the library and its good works that he expressed regret that he wasn't a librarian! I began to attend the weekly cabinet meetings of the manager, met the various city counselors, and became friends with city department heads and their assistants. Nor did I fail to cultivate the secretaries and other who make municipal government really function.

All of use are dealing with people. The secret is to develop warm, sincere, empathetic relationships with them. Then the magic is at work, day by day; the response, at critical times, is there when you need it. By way of example, the city contribution has grown from $3.60 to $9.54 per capita; the total budget has grown from $4.39 to $12.31 per capita.

Turning to the prospect of state aid as a source of funds, I searched the literature to find what other states were doing for their libraries. Then I wrote a "white paper" and saw to it that the state librarian, as well as others in the library community, seriously began to consider the ways and means of increasing state funding for libraries. Over several years, the striving entailed the efforts of many people, working cooperatively at different levels: librarians, legislators, lay persons. Portland now receives some $54,000 in state aid which we consider just a beginning. Nor do we neglect to see that we get our "fair share" of federal LSCA grants, distributed through the state library.

The quest for money is a multifaceted approach, and so it was with our quest for a new central library for Portland. It involved the support of the media. There were literally hundreds of articles about the need for a new library in the local press, along with on-going publicity on current programs and services. The quest involved several years of "bank-rolling" small increments of funds in each year's capital budget for site acquisition, architect fees, etc. It involved an ever-widening circle of total community involvement in the drive toward a new facility. In essence, it was a political process to establish the library as the *first* priority among many other urgent, pressing needs. Unswerving tenacity over a period of seven years was one of the prime factors in success. In Portland's case, the end result was a combination of federal, local, and private funds.

The quest for money never stops.When you reach temporary plateaus of funding from established sources, then perhaps you look for new sources. For example, when Portland's new library is completed in the spring of 1979, we plan to undertake an annual giving campaign by direct mail to supplement our yearly operating budget. We also plan to pursue foundation grants to fund cooperative projects with other libraries that participate with us in a regional library system.

Indirect sources of income are open to alert library managers. For example, the Comprehensive Employment Training Act (CETA) provides training opportunities for unemployed persons. For several years Portland has augmented its regular authorized staff by an additional 20 percent, utilizing CETA. These positions can employ all levels of library workers, from clerical to professional.We also take advantage of college "work-study" students, 80 percent of their wages being paid by cooperating institutions of higher education under a federal program. We also utilize special programs such as the Retired Senior Employment Program, which will furnish up to twenty hours of weekly employment for persons over fifty-five who meet the eligibility requirements.

In retrospect, if one of the key factors in successful library funding is the development of personal relationships, or rapport with decision makers and those who surround them, one begins with oneself and a constructive attitude even toward the opposition.

It is not easy to *like* your opponents, but it is *necessary*. One senior member of the city planning board adroitly stalled our efforts for a new library for two years. There were two options: one, do battle in anger and try to overwhelm the opposition; the other, win friendship and respect and hope to soften the opposition. In the end, we gained a staunch supporter and friend of the public library, but it wasn't easy. It took much patience and soul searching (if you will) to develop the continuing positive attitude that is essential for interpersonal relationships. But the *magic* is there, and the *magic* is *you!*

The Friends of Kresge Library, Oakland University

Robert G. Gaylor

Oakland University, Rochester, Michigan, is a four-year educational institution established in 1959. The campus proper and $2 million seed money were a gift from Mr. and Mrs. Alfred G. Wilson. She was the former Matilda R. Dodge, wife of one of the founders of the Dodge automobile company.

The Friends of the Kresge Library of Oakland University was established in March 1963. As the new school had tremendous needs and financial pressures, volunteer programs were promoted in every campus activity. The library was just one area that "required everything," and a volunteer group was formed to provide developmental funds.

Friends groups on academic campuses are new; most have been established since 1970. Of course, public libraries have long had such groups, and academic libraries, because of mounting financial pressures, are establishing friends groups with increasing rapidity.

The by-laws of the Friends of the Kresge Library of Michigan State University–Oakland (the university's former name) stated the group's purpose as to "support, promote, benefit, and participate in the activities, projects, and programs of the Library."

The university president, Woody Varner; director of community relations, June Matthews Bennett; and librarian, David Wilder, campaigned for the formation of such a group, and an enthusiastic group was established. The first persons to hold the office of president were Judge Carl and Libby Ingraham. In an attempt to win a broad base of community support, the formulators established a board of directors of twenty-one, and it has been the policy to elect couples to the board. A husband and wife may be elected to hold a single office or as a director. The board is quite large and supposedly representative of the community. The university president and the University Librarian are ex officio and nonvoting members of the board.

The officers of the association are a president, vice president, and secretary-treasurer, elected from the board for a one-year term. The board is elected at an annual membership meeting in May. The membership consists of anyone who pays his or her annual membership dues.

At present, the membership consists of some 400 individuals, with a complete roster of officers and directors. The large number of committees is indicated in the bylaws, such as Donations, Exhibit and Decorations, Acquisitions and Special Properties, Meetings and Activities, Membership, Nominations, Publicity and Public Relations.

Throughout the history of the friends, however, a number of these committees have ceased to exist or to function in the same capacity as originally specified in the bylaws. The board has the responsibility to fill the committee roster.

Over the years, the role of the friends has changed. In the beginning the group raised modest amounts of money and secured substantial gifts of books for the young library.

In the late '60s the friends group began a series of programs to enlighten its membership. At the annual friends dinner, held in the spring of each year, notable bookmen gave after-dinner speeches. Such individuals as Charles Feinberg, the noted Walt Whitman collector, and Richard Harwell, librarian at Bowdoin College, were invited.

In 1967 the library administration hired Peggy S. Pearce as executive secretary and the modus operandi of the organization changed again. The friends wished to make substantial contributions to the library book budget. Guest speakers and the acquiring of book collections were still a part of the friends' activities, but the new executive secretary came up with an "award winning" fund raiser, the Glyndebourne Picnic, in 1968. The annual picnic, on the estate of Matilda R. Dodge Wilson (the university's benefactress), was fashioned after the popular Glyndebourne Festival in England, where, each year, Mr. and Mrs. John Christie open their magnificent estate at Lewes (near Sussex) for the entertainment of Londoners, dressed in evening attire. Their guests bring picnics of food and wine or cocktails to dine on the grass while a famous opera is performed.

For the Oakland University version of Glyndebourne, the Friends of the Kresge Library transform the Indoor Riding Ring on the Meadow Brook Estate into a garden wonderland. Invited guests pay $50 to $100 a couple to bring their own food, liquor, and china and dine in the riding ring. A most elegant affair, it is the opening of the social season in metropolitan Detroit. Transforming the riding ring into a fabulous garden takes weeks and thousands of volunteer hours. Gardeners raise flowers in pots in the color scheme of the picnic. Florists and landscape gardeners are invited to share some of their talents around the theme selected each year by the executive board.

Honorary chairmen (prominent area citizens) are selected and lend their names to the prestige of the affair. Volunteers address and mail some 2,000 invitations. The capacity of the ring is 500, and in the past two years this capacity has been reached. Each year the chairmen are challenged to beat the record of the previous year, and they have succeeded (see the appendix at the end of this section). Expenses are held to a minimum as most items are obtained from corporations as gifts. The first year's proceeds of $2,100 have increased almost tenfold with the decade. The basic philosophy behind the idea was to develop a fund raiser that would be unique and could become socially prestigious.

The picnic caught on and surpassed its founders' wildest dreams. In 1976 the guests simply outdid each other, with little cost to the

Glyndebourne Picnic History
(Oakland University)

Year	Chairpersons	Theme	Attendance	Proceeds	Purchases for University Library
1968	Mr./Mrs. Lloyd H. Diehl, Jr.	My Fair Lady	125	$2,117	Early English literature, 16th and 17th centuries
1969	Mr./Mrs. George F. Pierrot	Camelot	250	2,700	Microfilm of New York Times through World War II
1970	Mr./Mrs. B. James Theodoroff	Brighton Pavilion	325	3,210	English literature of 18th century
1971	Mr./Mrs. Charles H. Allen	Ascot Races	487	6,331	Classics and history
1972	Mr./Mrs. Kenneth W. Cunningham	Oriental-English Mikado	480	8,300	Art and black studies
1973	Mr./Mrs. Leonard T. Lewis	Robin Hood's Sherwood Forest	490	10,056	Performing arts
1974	Mr./Mrs. Alan Loofbourrow	Henry VIII	500	14,000	Health sciences for nursing program
1975	Mr./Mrs. Mitchell I. Kafarski	Queen Victoria and Prince Albert's England	500	12,125	Slavic, Latin, Asian, African area studies
1976	Mr./Mrs. Richard Holmes	Shakespeare	485	20,000	Histories, documents, reference books

sponsors. They dressed in their best "bib and tucker," brought their best china and crystal, catered their foods (pheasant and truffles)—and the sponsors had only to provide tables, chairs, dance floor, orchestra (generally paid for by a sponsor), car parkers, and picnic-basket pages.

The picnic was covered by all the area media and the socially elite flocked to it. The services of a corporation's public relations department were secured and the press was invited to attend as guests. Those who are familiar with the way the press operates were greatly impressed with the press kits developed by the corporation's staff.

The automotive companies contributed greatly to the picnic and received due recognition in return. In past years the automotive companies have provided vans and trucks for transporting the flowers and props for the event. Automotive executives have loaned the skills and the time of their display managers and have persuaded other companies to supply needed services or equipment. A program, listing patrons and/or sponsors, appears prominently on each table at the event.

The Glyndebourne Picnic is a success—it raises the money for the library and is a unique, prestigious affair!

The Friends of Kresge Library bases its fund-raising efforts on this one event but sponsors, in addition, author and coffee hours or luncheons and the usual used-book sales. These affairs raise about a thousand dollars annually.

A new twist was developed for the annual dinner for the friends membership: to make available, for purchase at retail prices, those books the library had already paid for at wholesale prices. It demonstrated to the friends the cost of maintaining a good library collection. This event raises about a thousand dollars each year.

A speakers' bureau was established by the friends in 1970 to raise money for a particular faculty member's department. When a community group requests a speaker, arrangements are made by the friends, including the establishment of a proper stipend. After the faculty member speaks at the designated function, the stipend is directed by the library to purchase books for the faculty member's department or a selected subject matter.

The accomplishments of the friends have been many. Their loyal and devoted support has raised approximately $100,000 since their founding in 1963. As can be seen from the table, most of that support has come within the past decade.

A side benefit has been improved community relations. As a new institution, its relationship with the community needed strong positive support. The Glyndebourne Picnic, as a major social community event, has done just that. The Friends of Kresge Library has provided an important alternative source of funding for an academic library.

Performing Arts Research Center at Lincoln Center

Richard M. Buck and Thor E. Wood

The Performing Arts Research Center (PARC) of the New York Public Library at Lincoln Center is located within the most prestigious performing arts complex in one of the highest concentrations of performing artists in the world—the New York metropolitan area. Its location provides a number of advantages for fund raising through special events, for example, benefit performances and sales.

Since many of the center's regular users and visitors are highly visible and popular personalities, and loyal to the archives which contain permanent records of their careers, PARC has a large cadre from which to draw when planning a performance or a "celebrity" sale or auction. Experience shows that advance publicity and audience draw are greater if a few names from the social or performing areas are announced or talked about as planning to attend.

The New York metropolitan area audience is vast and varied. Almost any kind of performance is sure to draw if the price is right and the attraction is worthwhile. There is a sure-fire dance audience, theater audience, popular music audience, and classical music audience. Cutting across all these is the patron audience, whose loyalty to good causes includes almost all types of performances and events. Few cities in the world have as many wealthy individuals who are consistently willing to support a worthy charity by purchasing tickets.

Much of the New York area performance-going audience is also a memorabilia-collecting audience. Some collect valuable rare items and many more collect inexpensive trivia in quantity. Our bazaars appeal primarily but not exclusively to the latter, while the auctions appeal only to the former. We find that buyers come regularly from other parts of the East Coast as well. Because of the continuity of the events and the reputation for bargains that we have established, many collectors look forward to the bazaar day; some even complain if notice of the date has not come to their attention.

PARC's reputation and geographical location combine to make it the first choice for many when donating performing-arts material. These donations are extremely important for the development of the collections, since a large percentage of the collected original source material could not be purchased. However, many of the items (especially programs, librettos, souvenir books, periodicals, photographs, and posters) are already in the collections, and all the duplicates are turned over to the bazaar or auction sales. Since we accumulate such a large quantity just in these areas each year, and to reinforce the nature of the center, we limit the sale to performing-arts material. Other libraries that might be planning sales would not need to be as specialized.

There are also disadvantages associated with its location. Being located in the heart of a cultural capital has the disadvantage of competition with other events every time we organize a benefit performance. During the gala weeks of spring and fall, there are often four or five other galas and several charity balls in the same week. This means that the event must be particularly attractive and the invitation lists very strong to sell the tickets at benefit prices. The aim is to find the least competitive date, when the largest number of wealthy people are apt to be in town.

The New York metropolitan area is so saturated with celebrities and special events that a night when Jacqueline Onassis, Elizabeth Taylor, Mikhail Baryshnikov, Andy Warhol, and Tony Randall are all together, with most of them performing, becomes just another ho-hum evening for some celebrity followers. The press might not cover it until after the fact, and probably not the way the fund-raising organization would have wanted it covered. For the sake of the performers and to maximize sales, the publicity must be ready in advance, preferably several weeks in advance.

For this, one needs a "gimmick," something that makes news—a new pas de deux choreographed by Jerome Robbins, Baryshnikov's jeans to auction, Comden and Green selling sheet music—that can be played up in the press and television interview shows so that the potential audience will consider our event the one that must not be missed. Even with the gimmicks, the press must be constantly reminded that it is its duty to support PARC's cause and run stories and features. One has to believe strongly in one's cause in order to sell it to the media. The library's administration and the press office must feel that no cause is more worthy than ours and no event more worthy of attending, both for the cause and for the enjoyment or values it will bring.

Back in October 1971, which seems many more years ago than it is, the PARC staff were neophytes. When the PARC units were threatened with closing on January 1, 1972, if someone did not come up with a quarter of a million dollars, it tried something the New

York Public Library had never done before—a charity auction and exhibition-opening reception at a relatively small benefit admission price. With only a little experience from previous exhibition receptions, the administrative office worked with the Theatre Collection and a few volunteers to plan the event, which took place at the opening of a major exhibition honoring the Theatre Collection's fortieth anniversary. Under less than ideal conditions, in the Great Hall of the Central Building at 5th Avenue and 42nd Street, we held a cocktail party, had a celebrity auction, and sold memorabilia at two small tables. Although we netted only $7,000 (actually, a considerable success) from the auction, the word got around and the experience helped. The two small tables grew to the annual Giant Bazaar, the auctions have become more sophisticated, and the cocktail party has become decidedly secondary.

Even before the celebrity auction, it was realized that further efforts must be made to make PARC's plight more visible. With the administrative office as headquarters, a series of five 9 o'clock "Crisis Concerts" was organized, to be held in December 1971 and January 1972. Each of PARC's specialties was represented by performances in the building's 200-seat auditorium, and "An Evening with Comden and Green" was held in the large Juilliard Theatre next door. Again, the total net was not large (about $13,500), but the publicity was valuable, and the evening of dance (which was so successful it was performed twice in one night) led eventually to one of the greatest galas New York has ever seen.

Although many benefit performances followed the crisis concerts over the years, some produced through PARC/Administration and others by special arrangements, the Star Spangled Gala in May 1976 was the largest undertaking. Produced by James Lipton, the same person who was responsible for the "crisis" evening of dance, this performance at the Metropolitan Opera House has been called the "Gala Person's Gala" by Clive Barnes and was one of the greatest collections of talent ever assembled for an evening. PARC staff learned much from it and now is more aware than ever of the many problems of production and audience development that befall all benefit-producing organizations.

What follows is divided into three parts, each of which is outlined for ease of reference. First is a step-by-step accounting of all the elements which go into planning and staging a special fund-raising event at PARC. Second is a listing of some of the things experience in such fund-raising activities has taught and the procedures which over time have been developed to make the operations operate as smoothly as possible. Third is a highlighting of what other libraries can learn from the PARC experience.

PARC Planning and Implementing of Special Events

I. Who is involved

A. Administration

For special fund-raising events the planning is carried out by the PARC administrative staff, together with a few regular volunteers and the library's central administration. The plans are coordinated with the development and public relations offices. Much of the actual preparation is done by the adminstrative secretary and a corps of special volunteers recruited for the specific event.

B. Public relations

The library's public relations office has staff members, interested in the arts, who are able to get radio and TV coverage, as well as stories to the local press. Such an interest is vital in order to do the kind of pre-event promotion necessary to attract audiences to fund-raising events.

Other staff members and volunteers, working regularly on events, have developed working contacts among performers and publicity people on whom they call during the preparatory stages. Prominent people with drawing power can be very helpful with advance publicity and appearances at the event itself. Coordination of diversified activities of this kind in a central office is difficult to achieve but necessary.

C. Building staff

Without the active support of the building and maintenance staff, it would be impossible to conduct the library's fund-raising events. The building manager and his staff help in planning the logistics for the activities in the building and arrange for many kinds of special services.

D. Volunteer staff

With time and experience, it is possible to develop a core group of volunteers who will be available for special activities. It is very important in ongoing events to keep records of volunteers with various kinds of expertise and cumulated experience; otherwise, much time can be spent in training new workers. Volunteers can also be helpful in spreading the word to the specialized arts community and the community at large. The volunteer file includes names of people with various kinds of skills and abilities, ranging from envelope addressing and telephone reception to planning the event and requesting appropriate donations of materials.

II. What is done

Before anything is done, many factors of timing and quality must be considered in planning the event. Community calendars should be consulted in choosing a date. Long-range public relations value should be considered, along with actual money-raising potential; sometimes a small immediate net is less important than calling attention to the organization or the project. If the activity is to be an ongoing one, keep the quality high; disappointed people will not return.

A. Auctions and bazaars

1. *Materials.* All of the materials sold at PARC's bazaars and auctions are either duplicated in the collections or donated items that do not fit into the New York Public Library's collections policy (e.g., three-dimensional objects, memorabilia, and paintings).

Bazaar items range from 25¢ theater programs and photographs to books and posters sold for $10 to $25 and sometimes more; enough material is accumulated for a bazaar each year. More expensive items, from $25 book sets and first editions to $1,000 Mucha posters, are set aside for an auction, which is usually held in alternate years.

2. *Organization and production*

a) *Bazaars:* During the course of the year the PARC administrative staff meets from time to time with the bazaar chairwoman and her core staff of bazaar specialists (all volunteers). The date, always in the late fall, must be decided in the spring so that calendar clearances, printing, and scheduling for summer preparations can proceed. During the summer, a corps of volunteers, organized under subject specialists who are also volunteers, prepares the material for the sale. This includes sorting, pricing, and storing, all according to plans worked out by the specialists. In the early fall the committee meets with the building manager and works out the physical needs for the day of the sale.

For a deluge of 2,000 or more avid collectors into our premises for a seven-hour buying spree, we have learned that we need a smooth-running operation that includes experienced coat-check personnel, cashiers, stock and sales persons, and guards. The workers for the day itself are charted onto a master schedule and given specific assignments under area captains. By coordinating the whole operation for that day through a central command post, over 150 volunteer workers are usefully employed and find the day pleasurable and rewarding, knowing they have helped a worthy cause.

b) *Auctions:* The organization for an auction proceeds with that of the bazaar. Special, valuable items are set aside from the bazaar and held for the auction. We limit the number of lots to twenty-five or at most forty, and keep the quality high by being very selective. In general, materials are requested for the "Bazaar and Auction," leaving decisions to planners as to whether an item is more appropriate for one event or the other. "Begging" material from celebrities, who we then hope will be present at the auction as "salesmen" to spur on the bidding, is also important. A celebrity auction is different from the usual kind in that—by using celebrities to introduce items, perhaps say a few words about the needs and worth of the institution, and then encourage the bidding—each lot takes considerable time. It may be difficult to hold the event to two hours if twenty-five lots are auctioned under such circumstances. Toward the end of the organization period, a list of items to be auctioned is produced and mailed to potential buyers, and as many celebrities as possible from the various fields of performing arts are asked to attend and participate (these invitations usually must be followed by telephone calls).

We have used professional and nonprofessional but experienced auctioneers. The professional will conduct the auction in a business-like way, but the nonprofessional is more apt to wheedle a higher figure (and risk making the audience feel uncomfortable and possibly embarrassed). In either case, an auctioneer with experience is important to pace the event. A small admission fee is charged to weed the simply curious from the serious collectors. On the day of the auction, a small corps of specially picked volunteers act as celebrity hosts, ushers, spotters, lot carriers, and cashiers for pick-up at the end of the sale. The building staff arranges much of the physical logistics (an auction requires almost as much special planning, such as sound and staging, as a large bazaar).

3. *Audience.* For the bazaars and auctions, a following has been built up over the years by publicity, continuity and momentum, and reputation. For the bazaar and auction mailing lists, we combine our performing-arts "interest" list, the bazaar "interest" list, and comb all the dealer and collector lists available. Since many of the same people keep returning, it is a challenge to find new material for the collecting interests, and new ideas to gain attention and publicity. We charge a nominal admission fee of $1 to the bazaar. We have found that many

collectors are quite serious and spend hours sorting through the material. Although a basic order to the material is essential, many buyers enjoy sifting through stacks of material within their category of interest.

4. *Results*. Although the financial results of the bazaars and auctions have not been large in terms of the overall budget, results in publicity for the collections and increased interest in the library have been beyond measure. The bazaar receipts have risen from $8,400 to about $22,000, with most of the costs paid by the $1 per person admission. The auction proceeds have increased as we have made more careful lot selections. The 1975 auction of fifty-six lots (too many) grossed nearly $15,000, with costs under $1,000.

5. *Problems and solutions*. The major problems in organizing a bazaar or auction are preparing the material properly for the sale and planning the logistics of the day. Over the years, we have learned that the sorting, pricing, and packaging of the items for a bazaar must be made as routine as possible, and the methodology must be explained to all the volunteer workers. With each successive event, the problems have become fewer and less serious. Some of the solutions are:

a) Allow plenty of space for the buyers to move around each display table.

b) Allow browsing space (perhaps on a carpeted floor) for materials which buyers might wish to sort, such as programs and photographs. It may be necessary for the collector to look through the entire stock to find the ones he or she wants.

c) Make all buyers check their coats and bags (to help prevent theft) and have experienced checkroom personnel. You may find it desirable to have floorwalkers in strategic points to answer questions and to spot shoplifters.

d) Seal all parcels as they leave the cash registers.

e) Have more salespeople than you think really necessary to keep the table and shelves in order.

f) Have two or three subject experts in each field. Sometimes very knowledgeable questions are asked that a specialist can answer and thus raise buyer interest.

g) Have a very strong command-post staff who are able to solve floor problems firmly but without offense to the buyers. The command post is also essential in keeping the volunteers assigned and placed as needed.

B. Exhibition receptions

1. *Background*. PARC is able to have opening or preview receptions only when a donor is willing to contribute the costs. Neverthe-

less, we have several each year, to which we are able to invite (as well as other donors of money or materials) celebrities of the field, press, and potential friends and donors. Such an event can thus be helpful to thank those who have already helped and valuable for later fund raising. Their value in bringing people into the library and making them aware of its activities and vitality is incalculable.

2. *Promotion previews.* Sometimes the library is approached by book publishers or motion-picture producers who wish to tie our exhibition to a publication party or a preview screening. This kind of commerical connection can sometimes be helpful, but should only be considered if the product is one with which the library wishes to be associated and the staff time will be worth the possible result. In general, we decline such offers unless there is a direct connection with the library: an exhibition we would have had anyway or the publication of a book which was researched mainly from our materials.

3. *Benefit previews.* On a few occasions we have used the opening of an exhibition for a benefit and charged admission. The greatest problem is knowing whether the event can be prestigious enough to draw a paying audience. Such a reception has the fewest problems of any fund-raising activity that PARC accomplishes, but also brings in the least money (usually $5,000 or less). Ticket prices have ranged from $5 to $25, when a buffet supper was provided. Because it is recognized that people can see the same exhibition the following days and weeks without any charge, something unique or very special should be planned for the benefit preview.

4. *Organization.* The planning and organization, as well as the mailing list, addressing invitations, and selling tickets, are usually dependent on an outside committee of the Friends type. Personal notes which these people can add to the invitations help enormously (these notes can be best when brief and informal: "Helen—John and I hope to see you and Bob there—Mary," or "John and I hope you and Bob can join us for supper at our home before, and we'll all go to the library together"). The staffs of the units are also involved in the planning and detailed preparations, including the printing of invitations, and usually work with the key people of the committee. The PARC administrative staff acts in an advisory capacity and as liaison with the central administrative offices at 42d Street.

C. Galas and other performances

1. *Idea or concept.* PARC has now sponsored and/or produced five special benefits or galas at major houses, in addition to small benefit performances, some in the library's 212-seat auditorium. From the

beginning, we have found that a concept (a theme for an evening or series of evenings) around which to build the performance is the key to all the other aspects. We started small, and our original concept was to have all the varied performing arts join to save the library.

There are, after all, two alternative approaches one can use. The first is the choice of preproduced events (opening night of a "run" or a special single event produced in the normal course of any city's cultural activities) that would fit the library's image. The second is the creation, specifically for the library, of a one-night event or gala that would represent a range of the type of performing artists who need and use the facilities here. We prefer the latter, and it makes the development of a benefit performance more challenging.

2. *Production.* There is no production involvement on the part of the PARC staff if the performance is a prepackaged production. In that case, all our efforts go toward "audience development" (discussed under "4" below). However, in developing and producing a single performance gala, the staff and some of the corps of volunteers inevitably become involved with the production. Once the "concept" has been established, we have found that the production must be turned over to a professional producer, who in turn must work hand in hand with his library liaison. In finding the right producer, one must look for someone who knows how to find a production crew and performers who will present an evening worthy of selling, knows that production costs must be minimized, and above all knows the library and the problems we are trying to overcome by fund raising.

Once the production is under way, it is necessary to have continuous communication between all elements of the production proper and all of the supporting elements. We have tried several ways of doing this, but it seems most satisfactory to have one key person on each side to handle the day-to-day liaison between the producer and the central library administration, whether major conceptual or financial decisions are being made or if only for the myriad details. Production meetings (at least weekly toward the end) must be held at which all groups working on the event are represented. Many improvements in concept and program come only from face-to-face discussion of the evolving event.

3. *Performers.* Many artists in dance, music, and theater have become users and friends of PARC and have been willing to perform in benefits without asking for a fee. Both the quality and fame of the performer must be taken into account, as well as the size and scope of the concept. At first, we were content with artists who had less drawing power so long as they were friends of the library. We had little time to publicize, and if the artist would help with an evening

that would barely fill 200 seats, we were content to book him. One evening we had a concert of arias and small group pieces by the Metropolitan Opera Studio. None of the group was well known at that time, but among them was Frederica Von Stade, who has since become a leading soprano of both the Metropolitan and New York City opera companies.

As our benefit performances became larger (we do not want to use a house smaller than the Metropolitan now), we asked performers of greater stature. Because the roster of *Star Spangled Gala* in May 1976 included Mikhail Baryshnikov, Natalia Makarova, Peter Martins, Suzanne Farrell, Eugene Fodor, Paul Simon, Chita Rivera, and Gwen Verdon (among many others), there were lesser-known though greatly talented artist-friends of the library who asked to be in the Gala and had to be refused. It meant, of course, that everyone wants to join a successful event.

4. *Audience.* Audience development for large galas is as important as the program. In fact, it is continuous, while the gala production covers at most a six-month period. Over the years, the basic PARC list has been expanded to include every potential benefit patron whose name could be gleaned from any of the other patron and benefactor lists in New York City. And of course we always add to the file everyone who has purchased a ticket to any of our events. The basic list also includes friends of the New York Public Library who have been generous in other ways—by donations of money, materials, talent, or time.

The audience for a particular benefit performance varies, but for the major benefits that we now hold there is a basic group of patrons that has been developed over the years. Although these people are invited to become patrons for dozens of performances (for every charity) during the year, we find that they are uniformly loyal to the library. The less expensive tickets ($10 to $15) are sold very quickly from the general invitation mailing. We are not sure if the same people have come to many events, but our mailing list is so large (20,000-plus names) that enough people are interested to fill all the cheaper seats. We have purchased and exchanged lists to help the sales of the more expensive tickets, and are learning which lists draw and which do not.

5. *Results.* From the beginning, the results have been successful enough to make us feel that the continuance of benefit performances is worthwhile. In the early days of the concept, we were content with raising $5,000 to $10,000 for an evening, with almost no overhead. As expertise has increased, along with the need for funds, we feel that $50,000 to $75,000 must be raised per evening to make the elaborate

preparation worthwhile. Overhead increases tremendously with size, and it becomes difficult not to spend more than half of the gross income on the production costs. Had not the *Star Spangled Gala* suffered from gigantism, resulting in thousands of dollars in overtime costs, the costs in this case too would have been about half the gross. As it turned out, we netted about $85,000 on a gross of $190,000.

It must always be remembered that only the stars of a benefit perform free. All other union members are usually paid full salary, including overtime. This applies to members of all the performers' unions—theatrical, dance, musical—and all who are considered "nonstars" by the unions, who must be paid at least basic union scale (including film projectionists). Although many of the volunteer production staff work for nothing or expenses, the production cost of any large performance, at least in cities where performers' and stage hands' unions are powerful, will be very great. Without experienced or at least terribly energetic and eager staff members who can make the time to oversee, coordinate, and tend to the many details, it may be necessary to pay (on an "as needed" basis) a benefit coordinator. While this adds to the overhead costs of the event, you can expect certain standards of accomplishment which you cannot demand of a volunteer.

6. *Problems*. There are so many problems in mounting and selling a single-performance benefit (or even selling a block of tickets to a ready-made production) that there is room here to touch on only the most significant. The most difficult problem for any library is finding and choosing the right program—one that will produce the most revenue with the least effort and still be worthy of the institution. If the benefit orientation of the organization becomes known, offers to arrange benefits will be received in such number that refusing them will become a problem. Be wary of spreading the appeals too frequently or thinly; better to have one great evening than a half dozen small programs with little value, either for publicity or funds. It is often as much trouble to organize a small event as a large one.

For a performance produced by our library, another great problem is getting the right producer for the envisioned concept, and then working with the producer to get the performers and production staff. Another major problem is getting commitments from busy artists from whom many demands are constantly made. Musicians and concert performers are often partially booked two and three years in advance. On the other hand, film and stage actors are reluctant to make a commitment even six months ahead for fear an opportunity will suddenly emerge to make a movie or appear in a play with the potential for a long run. In general, we have found it much easier to convince artists that they should donate their time for our cause when we could speak with them directly (sometimes over a period of many months or even years). An artist's agent must be respected, but do not hope that he will take any interest in your case; his job is to find paying work for his client, not to give the client's talents away free.

Neither the institution nor the outside producer can have complete control, but the producer must be allowed final artistic or creative control within certain preestablished restrictions. It is very difficult for library administrators to understand theater people, and vice versa. The problem of finding liaison personnel who understand the minds of both types may be the most difficult of all.

Selling the attraction may or may not be a problem, depending upon the event, the community, and the goals set for the gross. For a maximum gross on a very high patron-benefactor ticket scale ($100–$250 each), great effort must be expended through personal appeals, letters, and invitations. On the other hand, a $5 or $10 top on a popular attraction in a small house sells rather easily—but does not gross much.

Other problems that eventually come up are proper (limited) use of press and free seats, how to reduce ticket prices to fill the house if sales are not going well (there are good and poor ways, and one must be careful), how to organize the finances of the production, whether and how to try to underwrite certain or all the costs, whether to spend proceeds for a patron or postperformance party, etc.

Even with years of experience, one cannot foresee all the problems of a particular event. A handbook on producing and selling such an event would be helpful, but it could not forewarn one of all the pitfalls that may be encountered.

Lessons Learned from Experience

I. Getting started

It is best to start small, and plan something you know you can accomplish within the limitations of purpose. The goal should come first, followed by the development of a program to meet it. In planning the program, call upon the expertise of community friends of the library and local talent, but beware of engulfment by eager friends and perforoers who may not be good enough for your purposes. Remember that success breeds success and that as you build up your reputation you can be more selective in activities and helpers.

II. Establishing procedures

At first, our fund-raising activities grew from desperation, and circumstances forced a hit-or-miss approach. As the events increased in size, procedures have been developed to make the operations as smooth as possible.

A. Bazaars and other sales

1. Gather and sort the material well in advance.

2. Establish—with competent, knowledgeable specialists—a basic pricing scale and method.

3. Use the most knowledgeable volunteers you can get to do the actual pricing.

4. Devise a coding method so that the contents of stored cartons are easily recognizable from the outside.

5. Set the sale date well in advance and prepare all publicity pieces for a six-week campaign.

6. Schedule all staff, aides, and celebrity guests into a master plan that can be coordinated and controlled from a central command post on the day of the sale.

7. Arrange detailed charts of the selling areas and all logistics well in advance, and plan for special signs and information guides that will be needed.

8. Orient all staff and aides to the floor plan and their areas of responsibility before the public is allowed to enter.

9. Safeguard books and other library property that are not for sale, and station security people at strategic locations. Have no unguarded exits.

10. Consider charging an admission donation, even if only $1, if you are apt to have a problem with the merely curious.

11. For auctions, circulate the list or catalog one month in advance, and allow mail or absentee bids.

12. Use professional auctioneers or an experienced amateur.

13. If you use celebrities, ask those who are "good at spontaneity," saving those whom you might later ask to give a benefit performance for another occasion.

14. For auctions, have a good cadre of spotters and lot carriers, and give them orientation training.

15. Arrange for pickup of lots during and/or immediately following the auction, and have an excellent cashier and packing staff at the pickup point, especially to handle checks and special arrangements.

B. Benefit performances

1. Establish the date, place, and concept early, preferably six to eight months before the performance. If you are "buying" a prepackaged evening, choose one at least four months ahead, and be as selective as you dare.

2. Set up production liaison within the library administration to work with (1) the actual producer of the program, (2) the audience development committee, and (3) the public relations office or staff.

3. Calendar the various aspects of the approaching event carefully and supply members of all committees with their appropriate schedule deadlines. Everything from printing deadlines to mailing of tickets should be carefully timed, although sometimes it is impossible to adhere strictly to the schedules.

4. Set up a careful budget framework and know who is to handle various aspects of the finances and who will be authorized to approve payments.

5. For major productions, a company manager with a separate production account is essential.

6. Know exactly how the ticket sales and mailings are to be handled, and draw up a list of procedures for phone calls, check posting and financial reporting that all who do the clerical work will be required to follow.

III. Keeping costs down

Establish production and audience development budgets early, listing all possible costs. Often some research must go into this, but what you find out at this stage is often helpful later. All who work on the event must know the budget for their aspect and not go over the limit without specific clearance from the library administration. The first rule of keeping costs down is to use as much volunteer help as possible. Another great saving is accomplished by getting free publicity through local publications and radio and TV stations as a public service. Paid advertising should be used only as a last resort.

If possible, try for underwriting. When a benefactor pays for all or part of the production costs in return for a listing in the program, a higher net is realized.

IV. Developing the audience

One of the most important aspects of building an audience is maintenance of an address file, to be used for invitations to benefits, auctions, exhibition openings, etc. Beyond this, you will want to develop and maintain "hot" lists of your most important prospects. How this is done depends on the circumstances, but over the years you will learn the key people who are most loyal to your cause and whom you will want to contact first when organizing the newest event. In some situations their names will be important in the formation of a patrons' committee and you will want to ask their permission to use their names before the invitation copy goes to press.

If your events are well received by the audiences and press, your ticket will become as "hot" as your list. The big spenders for galas ($100–$250 per seat) must be personally cultivated by letters and phone calls. This may involve a social committee or specially chosen volunteers who know many wealthy patrons personally. The media can help develop the audience that follows the celebrities and the stars (use the press in every way possible).

V. Keeping the public aware

Even between major fund-raising events, try to remind the publicthat you exist and are active. Invite potential patrons or buyers to any receptions or gallery openings appropriate to their interests, and be sure the press is aware well in advance of all library events. Before a major event, send invitations to the appropriate lists, timed so that former buyers get the word before the general public does. As your success grows, many people will ask to be added to the mailing lists.

Cultivate media people and try to get special advance stories by calling reporters and feature writers. However, do not depend on press releases alone; follow up on everything.

VI. Planning for continuity

For sales and performances, there is great value in continuity. Our bazaar has become an event that many look forward to each year, and repeat buyers account for a great part of the sales. Even keeping to the same general time of the year is valuable as part of keeping the event implanted in peoples' subconscious. The performance or event need not be held with such regularity, but our experience shows that after a success we are asked when the next benefit will be. Since the patrons are so important for a gala, the necessity of avoiding ronflicts (as well as getting the right performers) should take precedence over making the performance an annual spring or fall event. Some organizations *do* plan galas this way, but generally net less as a result.

VII. Saying "no"

A. To donations for sales

Because of the great accumulation of duplicates for bazaars, we have sometimes had to turn down donations simply because we could not handle the quantities. In order not to offend the donor, we explain why the gift must be declined and suggest they either hold the material for another year or give it to some other worthy organization. Remember—if you ever expect to have an auction, try not to turn down good items, no matter how difficult it is to store them; it may be difficult or impossible to make up the gap later. If you must turn something down, do so as tactfully as possible. It may be offered again when you can use it.

B. To potential benefits

Because of the success-breeds-success syndrome, we are offered live performances and film premieres that (usually for reasons of uncertain quality) we do not want to accept, and one has to be cautious in giving a reason for the turndown. We say that we feel the potential net from a benefit of this size would not be great enough to warrant our staff's promotion, that too many other events are planned at this time, or that the only benefits we are now contemplating are those the library itself puts together. If the benefit package is offered with no work on our part, except the use of the library's name in promotion, we are less prone to say no—so long as the event is not a total cultural zero or the library's name would be used solely because the event needs it to succeed.

C. To potential performers

When a gala is being programmed, there tends to be a bandwagon effect; after two or three stars are scheduled, lesser lights tend to ask to be added to the parade. Saying no can be very difficult, especially if the latter have performed before. The producer must handle each case on its merits, but the best answer is that the program is already too long (even if one is waiting for more stars to fall into line). Indeed, length is a very real and common problem, at least in New York City. Minor stars can be used at celebrity auctions or special fund-raising rallies, and once they have performed for you they should always be invited to events as friends of the library.

Most importantly, we have learned to maintain a balance among types of events and to keep constantly alert to the possibilities of using sales and special performances as fund-raising events.

What Others Can Learn

I. Know your limitations

Before attempting any kind of benefit performance or sale activity, survey your possibilities and work within the framework of your capabilities. Because PARC started small, it was able to build a reputation for success and draw attention to its activities.

Do not try to carry out grandiose plans without knowing the possible financial outcome. As a general rule, work only on projects that will cost no more than half of the expected gross—then work very hard to attain that expected gross, or more. Assume, however, that the program, the publicity, and the ultimate sales will not be as good as you hope. Overinflated expectations can lead to great disappointment and a tendency to avoid beginning the next project.

In each planned venture, study your case carefully. Weigh the work and cost against the potential net. As carefully as possible, judge the public relations value. Find all the local sources of talent and material that can be used for your particular event, and work with all the resources available, both inside and outside the library framework, to realize and promote your plan.

II. Know your sources

Check your various community service organizations for sources of volunteers and promotional aids. Following a success, help will come to you, but beware of suffering fools gladly; learn to pick and choose among all offers of help.

For program planning and administration, you may need to contact a professional service (even perhaps from some other city) that sends professional producers and directors around the country organizing local talent for benefit programs. For audience develop ment, you may be wise to hire a professional theater-party coordinator, but always try to find someone (paid or volunteer) who feels that the library is the most important charity in town and will work wholeheartedly, with great enthusiasm, toward your benefit goals.

For donations of materials, try to get free publicity from the local media, place signs in the library, etc. At first, be willing to accept anything you think you can sell. With experience, your donation acceptances can become more discriminating.

For pricing donations for sales, call upon the expertise of local collectors, gallery owners, or other specialists. Most collectors will want to buy some of the items they are pricing, but we have not found this to be a problem. Rather, it can be an incentive in getting them to volunteer to do the work (if there is a lot of it), but caution must be used that they do not preempt the best items, leaving only the lesser items for your sales.

III. Know your community

Depending on the community, audience interests will vary. We have found that large benefit-paying audiences exist in the New York area for every kind of program so long as the price is right. By evaluation of your concept and potential audience, try to establish the appropriate price scale to fill the house at the highest possible gross. Beware of overpricing the most expensive tickets, since reducing such prices is tricky and can cause unfavorable reactions. Organizations that are known to reduce prices at the last minute have a harder time selling the most expensive tickets at the full price.

Keep the prices of items somewhat under standard dealer prices—collectors love a bargain. Learn the kinds of collectors or bargain hunters in the community. General book sales are easier than specialized sales, but if you have a specialty, capitalize on it and use it to gain public awareness.

Use lists of prospective patrons or buyers from as many sources as possible and learn (from event to event) the drawing power of the various kinds of lists, and even the buying patterns of individual patrons and collectors on the lists.

Getting to know the patrons in all their aspects is vital to planning, and developing methods of predicting success is all important.

In Summary

1. Begin with what you have and where you are.
2. Develop a following.
3. Seek volunteer aid of the genuinely useful kind.
4. Expand your goals only as your ability to reach them grows.
5. Always plan with care; spend more time on this than you think you will need.
6. Keep records of everything important.
7. Try to make the next event bigger, better, or more unusual.
8. Establish continuity; past accomplishments can be lost by stagnation.
9. Build new events from old; capitalize on continuing ideas and concepts.
10. Learn from mistakes and do not be "turned off" by setbacks or complaints; they can be learning situations and occasions for productive improvements.

Contributors

Ellen Barata is Assistant to the Director for Personnel and Public Relations of the Ferguson Library in Stamford, Connecticut. She has been a newspaper reporter, city editor, and freelance writer. She has done public relations for numerous nonprofit organizations in Connecticut, including libraries.

Patricia Senn Breivik is Dean of Library Services at Sangamon State University in Springfield, Illinois. Before coming to Illinois in 1976, she served four years as Assistant Dean of the Pratt Institute Graduate School of Library and Information Science. While at Pratt, she developed and coordinated a three-day institute entitled "Fund Raising for Libraries." She has also directed annual conference programs on that topic at the New York Library Association in 1976 and the Illinois Library Association in 1977. Before entering the library profession, she worked in fund raising, first as Assistant Director of Charities for the Christian Herald Association and then as Administrative Secretary to the National Chairman of the Fifty Million Dollar Fund for Capital Improvement of the United Presbyterian Church in the U.S.A., where she met and first worked with E. Burr Gibson.

Richard M. Buck is Assistant to the Chief of the Performing Arts Research Center of the New York Public Library at Lincoln Center.

Since 1971 he has organized and been responsible in large part for three auctions and six bazaars, held to benefit the Performing Arts Research Center, and he initiated the PARC benefit programs ("Crisis Concerts") in 1971. Mr. Buck has been the library liaison on four major performance benefits between 1972 and 1976. With Mr. Wood, he wrote the case study Special Events Fund Raising by the Performing Arts Research Center at Lincoln Center in chapter 14.

Thomas R. Buckman is an educator with a background in university library administration and information science. He became President of the Foundation Center in 1971, after serving three years as Professor of Bibliography and University Librarian at Northwestern University in Evanston, Illinois. Earlier, he was Director of Libraries at the University of Kansas, as well as Director of the International Relations Office of the American Library Association. With Ms. Goldstein, he wrote chapter 11, "Foundation Funding."

Edward V. Chenevert has been Library Director of the Portland, Maine, Public Library since 1970. During the last seven years, Portland has tripled its budget, doubled its staff, built two new branch libraries, and initiated many new programs and services. At present, Portland is constructing a new $6 million central library. Mr. Chenevert worked at the Detroit Public Library before he returned to Maine in 1953 to enter the real estate business. He continued in the business world until 1970, when he became Portland's librarian. Mr. Chenevert wrote the case study "Fund Raising at Portland Public Library" in chapter 14.

Andrew J. Eaton has served as Director of Libraries at Washington University in St. Louis, Missouri, for twenty-five years. His article, which originally appeared in the September 1971 issue of *College & Research Libraries,* was the result of the earliest serious study of fund raising for libraries of which the editors are aware. The study was made possible by a 1969 CLR grant, which enabled Dr. Eaton to travel around the country to interview library directors and development officers concerning cooperative and fund-raising activities. Dr. Eaton's article, "Fund Raising for University Libraries," appears as chapter 13.

Robert G. Gaylor is a librarian at Oakland University in Rochester, Michigan. He is currently a board member of the Friends of Kresge Library at Oakland University, and has been closely involved in the planning of activities for the Friends of Kresge Library and in charge of arrangements for the annual Glyndebourne Picnic, which is its chief fund-raising event. Mr. Gaylor wrote the case study "The Friends of Kresge Library, Oakland University" in chapter 14.

E. Burr Gibson is Executive Vice President and Treasurer of Marts & Lundy Inc., a nationally known fund-raising counsel. Marts & Lundy clients include numerous libraries, colleges, hospitals, churches, and other community and civic organizations. Mr. Gibson is currently a director and member of the Executive Committee of the National Arthritis Foundation. Between 1947 and 1964 he worked for the National Foundation (March of Dimes). He was the keynote speaker and chief resource panelist at the Pratt Institute on Fund Raising for Libraries, as well as a program speaker and workshop leader on fund raising for libraries at the New York Library Association in 1976 and the Illinois Library Association in 1977.

Sherry E. Goldstein is Director of the Foundation Center's Associates Program. She has been with the Foundation Center and served in various capacities since June 1971. Currently, she administers a service program that provides selected information on grant-making foundations to approximately 700 fund-seeking organizations. More recently, she also became a managing editor of the center's new loose-leaf service, *Source Book-Profiles,* which provides in-depth reports on over 500 major U.S. foundations. With Mr. Buckman, she wrote chapter 11, "Foundation Funding."

Herbert G. Howard is Director of Development for the Massachusetts Eye and Ear Infirmary in Boston, Massachusetts. He was in charge of fund raising by direct mail for the Massachusetts General Hospital in Boston from 1968 to 1977, where he was concerned with use of the modern technique of computerized personalized direct mail for donor renewals and prospecting for new donors. The hospital's donor file increased from 20,000 to 150,000 during this period. Mr. Howard has served as a trastee of the Abbot Public Library in Marblehead, Massachusetts, and was one of the speakers at the Pratt Institute on Fund Raising for Libraries. He wrote chapter 7, "Direct Mail Solicitation."

Alice Ihrig is Director of Civic and Cultural Programs at Moraine Valley Community College in Palos Hills, Illinois. She has been an elected official in local government, active in political campaigns, and has lobbied on behalf of mental health legislation and of the Illinois Library Association, of which she is a past president. She has been a member of the American Library Association's Legislation Committee, served on the ALA Executive Board from 1974 to 1978, and is chairperson of the ALA Committee on the White House Conference. She speaks at workshops and seminars on the legislation/lobbying process throughout the country. Ms. Ihrig, a past legislative chairwoman and president of the League of Women Voters of Illinois, served as league observer to the Illinois Constitutional Convention. She wrote chapter 10, "Lobbying."

Donald A. Miltner is Vice President for Public Affairs at Lesley College in Cambridge, Massachusetts. In addition to counseling various organizations, he has served such institutions as Pratt, Fordham, and Columbia universities as chief advancement officer. In recent years his programs have received six major national program management awards, including the Total Development and Financial Support Program of the Year among American Colleges and Universities. Mr. Miltner, one of the speakers at the Pratt Institute on Fund Raising for Libraries, wrote chapter 4, "The Case Statement."

Ann E. Prentice is Director of the Graduate School of Library and Information Science at the University of Tennessee, Knoxville. She is a specialist in library governance, with emphasis on public libraries and finance, and has taught, consulted, and written in this area for several years. Dr. Prentice has applied for, and received, federal funds, state funds, and revenue-sharing funds for libraries and for her own research. In 1977 the American Library Association published her book *Public Library Finance,* and she was the principal author of *Library Services Now in New York* (Albany, 1978), a background paper for the Governor's Commission Conference on Libraries. She served four years as a library trustee and from 1975 to 1978 was a system trustee, dealing largely with policymaking as it affects governance and funding. Dr. Prentice wrote chapter 9, "Government Funding."

Thor E. Wood is Chief of the Performing Arts Research Center of the New York Public Library at Lincoln Center. He has been responsible for administering three auctions and six bazaars, benefiting the Performing Arts Research Center since 1971. Mr. Wood has been responsible in large part for the administration of four major performance benefits between 1972 and 1976. With Mr. Buck, he wrote the case study "Special Events Fund Raising by the Performing Arts Center at Lincoln Center" in chapter 14.

Selected Annotated
Bibliography

American Association of Fund-Raising Counsel, *Giving, USA: 1978 Annual Report*. New York: AAFRC, 1978.

> A compilation of facts and trends on American philanthropy for the year 1977. New edition is published each year.

Blanchard, Jr., Paul. *KRC Fund Raiser's Manual: A Guide to Personalized Fund Raising*. New Canaan, Conn.: KRC Development Council, 1974.

> A how-to-do-it manual on capital fund-raising campaigning, special project fund raising, annual giving, deferred giving, and foundation grantsmanship.

Ecclesive, Joseph A., ed. *KRC Handbook of Fund-Raising Strategy and Tactics*. Mamaroneck, N.Y.: KRC Books, 1972.

> Practical suggestions and many examples of fund-raising techniques taken from the KRC letter, a monthly exchange medium for ideas and information for fund raisers. The sections include: people and organization, direct mail, copy and graphics, the computer and fund raising, and general principles, practices, and viewpoints.

Flanagan, Joan. *The Grass Roots Fundraising Book: How to Raise Money in Your Community*. Chicago: Swallow Press, 1977.

> A compilation of how-to information, including a detailed analysis for choosing the event that is potentially the most profitable; what steps

173

should be taken and who should take them. Should be particularly helpful for school and small public libraries.

Hellman, Howard, and Karin Abarbanel. *The Art of Winning Foundation Grants.* New York: Vanguard Press, 1975.

Step-by-step detailing of procedure in securing foundation grants. Includes a discussion of the tools available to the grant seeker and a sample proposal.

Margolin, Judith B. *About Foundations: How to Find the Facts You Need to Get a Grant.* New York: The Foundation Center, 1975.

Step-by-step guide on how and where to search for information on foundations. Highlights reference tools produced and services offered by the Foundation Center.

Russell, John M. *Giving and Taking—Across the Foundation Desk.* New York: Columbia University Teachers College Press, 1977.

Experienced foundation director analyzes the interactions between institutions seeking grants and the foundations they approach. Good insights and good advice.

Seymour, Harold J. *Designs for Fund Raising.* New York: McGraw-Hill, 1966.

Firsthand information on the principles, patterns, and techniques of fund raising by the dean of the fund-raising profession.